BOOKS BY CAROLYN KREITER-FORONDA

Contrary Visions (1988)

Gathering Light (1993)

Death Comes Riding (1999)

Greatest Hits, 1981 – 2000

River Country (2008)

The Embrace: Diego Rivera and Frida Kahlo (2013)

Seasons of Sharing: A Kasen Renku Collaboration (2014)
Carolyn Kreiter-Foronda and Joyce Brinkman
with Catherine Aubelle, Flor Aguilera García, Gabriele Glang,
and Kae Morii

ANTHOLOGIES

In a Certain Place (2000)
Edited by Carolyn Kreiter-Foronda and Alice Marie Tarnowski

Four Virginia Poets Laureate: A Teaching Guide (2006)
Edited by Carolyn Kreiter-Foronda and Edward W. Lull

Urban Voices (2014)
Edited by Carolyn Kreiter-Foronda and Joyce Brinkman

Copyright © 2018 Carolyn Kreiter-Foronda

All rights reserved. This book or any portion thereof may not be reproduced or used in any manner whatsoever without the express written permission of the publisher except for the use of brief quotations in a book review.

Editor: Robert P. Arthur

Cover and Book Design: Jeff Hewitt

Cover Painting: Carolyn Kreiter-Foronda, Iris, Lift Your Spirit to the Sun

Cover photograph: Michael Kunzinger

First printing, 2018

ISBN: 978-0-9968350-3-9 (Paperback)

San Francisco Bay Press
522 Spotswood Ave C5
Norfolk, Va, 23517

Sanfranciscobaypress.com

THESE FLECKS OF COLOR

New and Selected Poems

[1983 – 2017]

Carolyn Kreiter-Foronda

SAN FRANCISCO BAY PRESS • 2018

ACKNOWLEDGMENTS

The author extends appreciation to Harry N. Abrams, Inc., to Dover Publications, Inc., and to Marquand Books, Inc. for granting permission to use quotations from these sources:

THE DIARY OF FRIDA KAHLO English translation copyright ©1995 by Harry N. Abrams, Inc. [Used by permission of Harry N. Abrams, Inc., New York. All rights reserved.]

Rivera, Diego. *My Art, My Life: An Autobiography (with Gladys March).* Mineola, New York: Dover Publications, Inc., 1991, pp. 41 and 83. ISBN: 0-486-26938-8

Zamora, Martha. *Frida Kahlo: The Brush of Anguish.* Trans. Marilyn Sode. San Francisco: Chronicle Books, LLC, © 1990, p. 126. [Used with permission of Marquand Books, Inc., Seattle, WA]

The author expresses grateful appreciation to the editors of the following periodicals in which these poems, or earlier versions of them, first appeared:

CONTRARY VISIONS

All of the poems from *Contrary Visions* by Carolyn Kreiter-Kurylo, copyright ©1988, are reprinted by permission of the author. Note: The book was originally published by Scripta Humanistica under the name Carolyn Kreiter-Kurylo. The author's current name is Carolyn Kreiter-Foronda.

These poems or earlier versions of them first appeared in the following periodicals and anthologies:
Antioch Review: "From a Café Window, Tangier"; *Best New Poets of 1986:* "Touching a Stained-Glass Window in Gloucester Cathedral"; *Card Party:* "The Mathematical Bridge, Cambridge"; *Passages North:* "Crows over the Fields of Auvers"; *Phoebe:* "Contrary Visions in the Gallery, *White on White*," "Gifts"; *Poet Lore:* "What You Hear in a Studio,"

"Forgive Me, But This is Just a Smear of Purple," "The Peasant Woman above Tarifa," "At the Lawn Party"; *Prairie Schooner:* "Dream: Catching the Air"; *Sun Dog* (currently *The Southeast Review*): "The Aura," Baiting My Hook, I Try Again"; *The Federal Poet:* "The Blind Woman, 1967"; *The Mystic Muse:* "Spell of Moon and Maple"; *Visions International:* "From the Cloister, Saint-Rémy," "In the Hills of Les Baux"; *Wind/Literary Journal:* "Touch"

"Contrary Visions in the Gallery, *White on White*" was reprinted in *Greatest Hits 1981-2000* and in *Four Virginia Poets Laureate (2004-2012),* edited by Sofia Starnes (Cedar Creek Publishing, ©2013). The poem received first-place awards from *Phoebe* (1981) and *Spree* (1984-85) and was featured in *Riverstone* (Poets of the Foothills Arts Center).

"Crows over the Fields of Auvers" was reprinted in *Greatest Hits 1981-2000.*

"Nude Descending in All Directions" was reprinted in the Museum issue of *Beltway Poetry Quarterly.*

"Baiting My Hook, I Try Again" was anthologized in *The Journal of the Virginia Writing Project,* as well as in the Other Voices International Project's *Cyber-Anthology* and in *Sporting Words Anthology.* The poem also appears in *A Chesapeake Celebration* and was presented in dramatic performances by the Playwrights Premiere Theatre of New York and Virginia.

"Gifts" was reprinted in *Bay Splash.* It was anthologized in *Joys of the Table* (Richer Resources Publications, ©2015) and in *The Sound of Poets Cooking* (Jacar Press, ©2010).

GATHERING LIGHT

All of the poems from *Gathering Light* by Carolyn Kreiter-Foronda, copyright ©1993, are reprinted by permission of author. The book was originally published by SCOP Publications, Inc., which is archived at the University of Maryland.

These poems or earlier versions of them first appeared in the following periodicals:

Antietam Review: "When Birds Speak"; *Hispanic Culture Review:* "Something of Myself," "Machu Picchu," "Christmas in Bolivia," "Mariano Quispe"; *Lip Service:* "Beneath Lamplight" (previous title: "The Potato Eaters"); *Poet Lore:* "You Don't Need Binoculars to be a Bird Watcher"; *South Florida Poetry Review:* "Above Clouds"; *The Monserrat Review:* "As a Teacher I'm Inclined to Ignore the Critics," "Red Poppy"; *Virginia Writing:* "Among the Ruins of Puca Pucara, Perú," "In a Field by Lake Titicaca"

"Beneath Lamplight" was reprinted in "Spreading the Joy of Poetry," a news article by Bill Lohmann in the January 14, 2007 edition of the *Richmond Times-Dispatch*.

An excerpt of "You Don't Need Binoculars to Be a Bird Watcher" is featured in a permanent art installation by Martin Donlin as part of the Washington Metropolitan Area Authority, Art in Transit. The poem also appears in the anthology, *In a Certain Place,* co-edited by the author and Alice Marie Tarnowski (SCOP Publications, Inc., ©2000). It is reprinted in *Four Virginia Poets Laureate (2004 –2012).*

"Balloon Safari over Masai Mara" appears under the title, "At these Heights" in *WPFW 89.3 Poetry Anthology*, edited by Grace Cavalieri (The Bunny and the Crocodile Press, Washington, D.C., ©1992.)

"Christmas in Bolivia" was reprinted in the December 2008 issue of *The Dead Mule School of Southern Literature*.

DEATH COMES RIDING

All of the poems from *Death Comes Riding* by Carolyn Kreiter-Foronda, copyright ©1999, are reprinted by permission of author. The book was originally published by SCOP Publications, Inc., which is archived at the University of Maryland.

These poems or earlier versions of them first appeared in the following periodicals and anthologies:

BlackWater Review: "Ice Maiden"; *Blood to Remember: American Poets on the Holocaust,* first edition: "Leaving a Country Behind"; *Dominion Review:* "Katherine Anne Porter's Secret"; *Educational Travel Review:* "Transparent Butterfly in Jardín de Mariposas"; *Hispanic Culture Review:* "The Quechuan Boy of Cuzco" (previous title: "Marcus Antonio"), "Song to the Sun God, Inti," "In the Stonecutter's Workshop"; *Poetic Voices without Borders 2:* "Elena Mesa," "The Inca Dolls"; *The Other Voices International Project* cyber-anthology: "All Saints' Day"; *Virginia Writing:* "A Basket of Potatoes," "Vigil," "The Sacred Valley," "Azucena's Arpillera"

Excerpts from *Death Comes Riding* appear in *River Country: A Poem/Play*, dramatized by Robert P. Arthur with music by Amber Wood.

"A Basket of Potatoes" was reprinted in *Four Virginia Poets Laureate (2004 – 2012).*

"Mother" was anthologized in *After Shocks: The Poetry of Recovery for Life-Shattering Events,* edited by Tom Lombardo (Sante Lucia Books, ©2008).

"Katherine Anne Porter's Secret" was reprinted in the *Katherine Anne Porter Society Newsletter.*

"All Saints' Day" was reprinted in the anthology, *Poetic Voices without Borders 2,* edited by Robert L. Giron (Gival Press, ©2009.)

"Leaving a Country Behind" was reprinted in the second edition of *Blood to Remember: American Poets on the Holocaust,* edited by Charles Adés Fishman (Time Being Books, ©2007).

"Elena Mesa" was performed in *The Haunting: Tales for All Hallows* at 40th Street Stage in Norfolk, VA.

"The Sacred Valley" was reprinted in *BlackWater Review* and

The Pen Woman.

"The Quechuan Boy of Cuzco" was reprinted in *The Northern Virginia Review.*

"Azucena's Arpillera" was reprinted in the *4th Grade Virginia SOL Daily Reading Reviews,* edited by Jenny Funk and Margaret Thompson (THUNKS, Inc., ©2007).

An earlier version of "The Inca Dolls" was reprinted in *El Locofoco,* as well as in *Greatest Hits* (Pudding House Publications, ©2001); the *80th Anniversary Anthology* of the Poetry Society of Virginia (Warwick House Publishing, ©2003); and *In a Certain Place* (SCOP Publications, Inc., ©2000). The poem was nominated by Chapultepec Press for a Pushcart Prize XXII.

"In the Stonecutter's Workshop" was reprinted in *The Journal of the Virginia Writing Project.*

GREATEST HITS 1981–2000

All of the poems from *Greatest Hits 1981–2000* by Carolyn Kreiter-Foronda, copyright ©2001, are reprinted by permission of author. The book was originally published by Pudding House Publications as an invitational series and is archived at Ohio State University Libraries.

"Moonwatch" first appeared in *Radishes & Flowers: A Wallace Stevens Feast* and received a First Place Award in the 1981 Nationwide Poetry Contest of the National League of American Pen Women. The poem was reprinted in *The Cooke Book: A Seasoning of Poets* and in *Poems of the Super Moon.* It was featured on the NLAPW website.

"Donna Bruna" first appeared in *Day Tonight / Night Today* and in the author's collection, *Contrary Visions.* The poem was anthologized in *Montpelier: Plus 4, 1980-1984* and *In a Certain Place.*

"The Replica" first appeared in *Mid-American Review* and in the author's collection, *Contrary Visions*.

"Lately I Have Been Too Wrapped Up" first appeared in *Poet Lore* and in the author's collection, *Contrary Visions*. The poem was reprinted in the *Anthology of Magazine Verse & Yearbook of American Poetry (1985)*; the *80th Anniversary Anthology* of the Poetry Society of Virginia; and the *Cyber-Anthology* of the Other Voices International Project.

"Apples" first appeared in *Prairie Schooner* and in the author's collection, *Contrary Visions*. It was reprinted in *Four Virginia Poets Laureate (2004-2012)* and in *Spree*. "Apples" was also highlighted in *Virginia Living* ("Pieces of Wisdom" by Bill Glose) and anthologized in *Joys of the Table: An Anthology of Culinary Verse,* edited by Sally Zakariya.

"Do You Know about the Rain Tree?" first appeared in *Antietam Review* and in the author's collection, *Gathering Light*. It was nominated for a Pushcart XIX Prize by *Antietam Review* and reprinted in *Terrain.org: A Journal of the Built + Natural Environments*, Issue 21, Winter/Spring 2008. It was selected by Walter Cummins for *Best of the Literary Journals*, 2008, and by Roger Humes for the *Cyber-Anthology*.

"Stones" first appeared in *Antietam Review* and in the author's collection, *Death Comes Riding*.

"Among Cedars" first appeared in *BlackWater Review* and in the author's collection, *Death Comes Riding*. The poem was reprinted in *Southside Sentinel, The MacGuffin, The Pen Woman, Gloucester-Mathews Gazette Journal, A Common Wealth of Poetry*, and in *The Far West End Press*.

"On Sturgeon Creek" won The Poetry Society of Virginia's Edgar Allan Poe Memorial Prize in 1993. The poem first appeared in the author's collection, *Gathering Light* and was reprinted in The Poetry Society of Virginia's *80th Anniversary Anthology of Poems*, edited by Joe Awad, 2003.

RIVER COUNTRY

All of the poems from *River Country* by Carolyn Kreiter-Foronda, ©2008, are reprinted by permission of the author. The book was published by San Francisco Bay Press. Poems from the book appear in *River Country: A Poem/Play*, dramatized by Robert P. Arthur with music by Amber Wood.

These poems or earlier versions of them first appeared in the following periodicals and anthologies:

Bay Splash: "Blood Moon," "Raking the Blues," "The Jenny Dawn"; *Image/Word: A Book of Poems:* "The Deserted Beach"; *Kadmos Paris Anthology:* "Nest Building"; *Nimrod International Journal:* "These Flecks of Summer," "Hurricane"; *Southside Sentinel:* "Dragon Run"; *The Clinch Mountain Review:* "Crossing a Rappahannock River Bridge," "The Bay's Tributaries"; *The Dead Mule School of Southern Literature:* "Caught Littering by the Law," "Green Burial"; *The Poet's Domain:* "Hay Bales, Deltaville," "Elegant Worms," "Deforestation"; *Virginia Adversaria:* "Elves"; *Virginia Writing:* "By the Bay" (previous title: "By Tulum's Sea"); *Visions International:* "On the Studio Boat"

A Spanish translation of "The Deserted Beach" appears in the anthology, *Cauteloso engaño del sentito*, edited by Rei Berroa, as part of *Colección Libros de la Luna*, Vol. No. 2, Dominican Republic. An excerpt of the poem is featured in a permanent art installation by Martin Donlin at the McLean Metro Station in Northern Virginia as part of the Washington Metropolitan Area Authority, Art in Transit.

"Nest Building" received a First-Place award in the Chesapeake Bay Branch of the National League of American Pen Women writing competition and was translated into Spanish by Rei Berroa for the anthology, *Cauteloso engaño del sentito*.

"Dragon Run" was reprinted in the *Dragon Run Newsletter* and in *WORLD POETRY Yearbook 2015*. An excerpt of the poem appears in a DVD, *The Dragon Run: A Step into the Past / A Strategy for the Future,* produced by EAF Custom Communication.

"Elves" was nominated by the editors of *Virginia Adversaria* in 2001 for a Pushcart Prize.

"On the Studio Boat" was anthologized in *Cabin Fever: Poets at Joaquin Miller's Cabin, 1984 –2001,* edited by Jacklyn W. Potter, Dwaine Rieves, and Gary Stein (The Word Works, Washington, D.C., ©2003).

"These Flecks of Summer" was reprinted in the *Cyber-Anthology* in 2008 as part of the Other Voices International Project.

A Spanish translation of "Solitude" appears in the anthology, *Cauteloso engaño del sentito*, edited by Rei Berroa. The poem was reprinted in *Bay Splash* and in *Four Virginia Poets Laureate (2004 –2012).*

"Hay Bales, Deltaville" was reprinted in the PSV newsletter, *A Common Wealth of Poetry.*

"Blood Moon" was presented in the dramatic production, *The Haunting: Tale for All Hallows,* compiled by Robert P. Arthur and Hollis Pruitt and held in 2007 at 40th Street Stage in Norfolk, Virginia.

A Spanish translation of "Raking the Blues" appears in *Cauteloso engaño del sentito.*

"By the Bay" was reprinted in *Bay Splash* and *Four Virginia Poets Laureate (2004 –2012).* The poem was presented in a dramatic production, *Roses so Red and Lilies so Fair,* created and directed by Robert P. Arthur.

"Crossing a Rappahannock River Bridge" was featured in the *Cyber-Anthology.* In 2008, it was nominated by San Francisco Bay Press for a Pushcart Prize.

"Elegant Worms" was reprinted in *The Feminist Underground*.

"The Revenant on Lover's Lane" was reprinted in L. B. Taylor's book, *The Ghosts of Virginia,* Vol. XIII.

"Hurricane" was anthologized in *Four Virginia Poets Laureate (2004-2012).*

A Spanish translation of "The Bay's Tributaries" appears in *Cauteloso engaño del sentito*, edited by Rei Berroa. The poem was anthologized in *Weatherings,* edited by David Chorlton and Robert S. King.

"Green Burial" was presented in the dramatic production, *The Haunting: Tale for All Hallows.*

THE EMBRACE: DIEGO RIVERA AND FRIDA KAHLO
Winner of the 2014 Art in Literature: Mary Lynn Kotz Award

All of the poems from *The Embrace: Diego Rivera and Frida Kahlo* by Carolyn Kreiter-Foronda, copyright ©2013, are reprinted by permission of the author. The book was published by San Francisco Bay Press.

These poems or earlier versions of them first appeared in the following periodicals and anthologies: *An Endless Skyway: Poetry from the State Poets Laureate:* "Leaving the Mine," "The Two Fridas (II): Collage, Manhattan," "The Two Fridas (VII): Paint Me Flying"; *Apropos Literary Journal:* "Hymn: The Embrace," "The Two Fridas (I): On the Border Line between Mexico and the United States"; *Autumn Sky Poetry:* "Frida Dialogues with Her Heart"; *Connotation Press: An Online Artifact:* "Offerings, Day of the Dead," "Frida Kahlo," "Bread"; *Cutthroat: A Journal of the Arts:* "The Crematorium at the Panteón Civil de Dolores"; *Fjords Arts and Literary Review:* "The Two Fridas (VI): Broken Column and Plaster Cast," "La Casa Azul"; *Nimrod International Journal:* "Diego and Calla Lilies," "Halley's Comet"; *Poet Lore:* "The Two Fridas (III): Sitting on a Wicker Bed with Ceramic Doll."; *R.kv.r.y. Quarterly Literary Journal:* "Frida and Wet Nurse"; *The Comstock Review:* "The Two Fridas (IV)"; *The Poet's Domain:* "Letter to Diego";

Tipton Poetry Journal: "Entering the Mine," "The Two Fridas (V): The Wounded Table"

"Diego and Calla Lilies" was reprinted in the anthology, *An Endless Skyway: Poetry from the State Poets Laureate,* edited by Caryn Mirriam-Goldberg, Marilyn L. Taylor, Denise Low, and Walter Bargen. The poem was also selected for the anthology, *Aesthetica Creative Writing Annual* and anthologized in *Four Virginia Poets Laureate (2004-2012).* The poem was featured in a video in the Public Poetry Series.

"Bread" was reprinted in *Delaware Poetry Review* and anthologized in *Joys of the Table* (Richer Resources Publications, ©2015).

"Frida and Wet Nurse" was nominated by *R.kv.r.y. Quarterly Literary Journal* for a Pushcart Prize.

"The Two Fridas (IV)" received Special Merit recognition from *The Comstock Review.* The poem was reprinted in *Four Virginia Poets Laureate (2004-2012).*

"The Two Fridas (VI): Broken Column and Plaster Cast" was nominated by *Fjords Arts and Literary Review* for a Pushcart Prize.

"Letter to Diego" was translated into Spanish by Rei Berroa and anthologized in *Cauteloso engaño del sentido.*

"The Crematorium at the Panteón Civil de Dolores" was a finalist in the 2010 Joy Harjo Poetry Prize contest. The poem was reprinted in *Connotation Press: An Online Artifact.*

NEW POEMS

These poems or earlier versions of them first appeared in the following periodicals and anthologies: *Apropos Literary Journal:* "Northern Lights"; *Art Meets Literature: An Undying Love Affair:* "Femme Fatale," "Moonlight Marine"; *Crosswinds Poetry Journal:* "Miracle Flower"; *Delaware Poetry Review:*

"Tinnitus"; *Nimrod International Journal:* "Painting in an Enclosed Field at Saint-Paul Hospital"; *Hearts and Minds:* "Peace Offering"; *SLAB (Sound and Literary Art Book):* "Nine Lives"; *The Broadkill Review* (Poet Laureate Issue): "Claude Monet's Garden," "Evening Star," "Talisman for Discovery"; *The Fourth River:* "Fireflies"; *The Ledge:* "Seascapes"; *The Poet's Domain:* "Poplars on the Epte"; *Thirty Three Anniversary Anthology* (Negative Capability Press, ©2014): "O'Keeffe's Desert Terrain, Ghost Ranch"; *Visions International:* "Dipping My Brush into Black"; *World Poetry Yearbook 2015:* "Books," "In Polar Waters"

"Painting in an Enclosed Field at Saint-Paul Hospital" was reprinted in *Poetry Virginia Review.*

"Miracle Flower" was reprinted in the *VWC 100th Anniversary Anthology.*

"The Birth Night Ball," "A Midsummer Evening on the Piazza," and "A Private Place" are included in the archives of the Fred W. Smith National Library for the Study of George Washington and are featured in a video of a Virginia Poets Laureate Tea and Fellowship event, held at Mount Vernon in April 2016 (mountvernon.org).

"Books" was featured on the back cover of *World Poetry Yearbook 2015.*

"Tinnitus" was anthologized in *Rappahannock Voices* (Riverside Writers, ©2014).

"Peace Offering" was reprinted in *The Dead Mule School of Southern Literature.*

I express my heartfelt appreciation to my husband, Patricio Gómez-Foronda, for his continued support of my work as a poet and artist, as well as for serving as my translator during research trips to Spain, Mexico, Central and South America. I am indebted to my editor, Robert P. Arthur, for his insightful critiques and for producing and presenting poem/plays, based on portions of *Death Comes Riding* and *River Country.* I am grateful to Jeff Hewitt for his avid support and expertise in designing the book's layout and cover; photographer, Michael Kunzinger, for his artful rendition of my painting, *Iris, Lift Your Spirit to the Sun*; Cathryn Hankla for her generous endorsement on the book's cover; and Nancy Powell and Ann Shalaski for their perceptive critiques and steadfast support.

For Patricio Gómez-Foronda

CONTENTS

From *Contrary Visions*

Contrary Visions in the Gallery, *White on White*	1
From the Cloister, Saint-Rémy	2
Crows over the Fields of Auvers	4
Nude Descending in All Directions	6
The Mathematical Bridge, Cambridge	8
Touching a Stained-Glass Window in Gloucester Cathedral	10
The Aura	11
What You Hear in a Studio	12
Forgive Me, But This is Just a Smear of Purple	13
The Peasant Woman above Tarifa	14
From a Café Window, Tangier	15
In the Hills of Les Baux	16
Spell of Moon and Maple	17
Baiting My Hook, I Try Again	18
Dream: Catching the Air	20
The Blind Woman, 1967	22
At the Lawn Party	23
Touch	24
I Don't Know Why I Wake Up Angry	25
The Visiting Poet, Washington, D.C.	26
Gifts	27

From *Gathering Light*

As a Teacher I'm Inclined to Ignore the Critics   31

Red Poppy   32

Above Clouds   33

Beneath Lamplight   34

In Rodin's Studio at Meudon   35

Father   37

The Hibiscus   38

You Don't Need Binoculars to be a Bird Watcher   39

Balloon Safari over Masai Mara   40

When Birds Speak   41

The Rosetta Stone   42

Something of Myself   43

Among the Ruins of Puca Pucara, Perú   45

Machu Picchu   46

Christmas in Bolivia   48

Mariano Quispe   49

In a Field by Lake Titicaca   50

From *Death Comes Riding*

The Healing   55

The Telephone Ring   56

Mother   57

Katherine Anne Porter's Secret   59

All Saints' Day	61
Fifth Wife, Hampton Court Palace	63
Vigil	64
The Anne Frank House at Prinsengracht 263	65
Leaving a Country Behind	66
Ice Maiden	68
Elena Mesa	70
The Sacred Valley	71
The Quechuan Boy of Cuzco	72
Azucena's Arpillera	73
The Inca Dolls	74
A Basket of Potatoes	75
Song to the Sun God, Inti	76
Transparent Butterfly in Jardín de Mariposas	77
In the Stonecutter's Workshop	78

From *Greatest Hits 1981 –2000*

Moonwatch	83
Donna Bruna	85
The Replica	87
Lately I Have Been Too Wrapped Up	89
Apples	90
Do You Know about the Rain Tree?	91
Stones	93

Among Cedars — 94
On Sturgeon Creek — 95

From *River Country*

The Deserted Beach — 101
Nest Building — 103
Dragon Run — 104
Elves — 105
On the Studio Boat — 106
These Flecks of Summer — 107
Solitude — 110
Hay Bales, Deltaville — 111
Blood Moon — 112
Raking the Blues — 113
By the Bay — 114
Crossing a Rappahannock River Bridge — 115
Elegant Worms — 117
The Jenny Dawn — 120
The Revenant on Lover's Lane — 122
Hurricane — 125
The Bay's Tributaries — 126
Caught Littering by the Law — 127
Deforestation — 128
Green Burial — 130

From *The Embrace: Diego Rivera and Frida Kahlo*

DIEGO RIVERA

Diego and Calla Lilies 137

Halley's Comet 138

From: Murals

    I. Entering the Mine 141

    II. Leaving the Mine 142

    III. Hymn: The Embrace 144

    IV. Offerings, Day of the Dead 145

    V. Bread 146

Wives

    I. Angelina Beloff 148

    II. Lupe Marín 149

    III. Frida Kahlo 150

    IV. Emma Hurtado 151

FRIDA KAHLO

Frida and Wet Nurse 155

The Wedding Fiesta 156

The Two Fridas (I): On the Border Line between Mexico and the United States 158

The Two Fridas (II): Collage, Manhattan 159

The Two Fridas (III): Sitting on a Wicker Bed with Ceramic Doll	161
Frida Dialogues with Her Heart	162
The Two Fridas (IV)	164
The Two Fridas (V): The Wounded Table	165
The Two Fridas (VI): Broken Column and Plaster Cast	167
The Two Fridas (VII): Paint Me Flying	169
Letter to Diego	170
The Crematorium at the Panteón Civil de Dolores	172
La Casa Azul	174

NEW POEMS

These Flecks of Color	179
Painting in an Enclosed Field at Saint-Paul Hospital	180
Northern Lights	182
Femme Fatale	184
Moonlight Marine	185
Poplars on the Epte	186
Seascapes	187
Claude Monet's Garden	189
O'Keeffe's Desert Terrain, Ghost Ranch	190
Evening Star	191
Miracle Flower	192

George Washington: Mount Vernon

    I. The Birth Night Ball   193

    II. A Midsummer Evening on the Piazza   194

    III. A Private Place   195

    IV. The Final Battle, 1799   196

Dipping My Brush into Black   197

Nine Lives   198

Books   199

Talisman for Discovery   200

Tinnitus   201

Fireflies   203

In Polar Waters   204

Have Mercy   205

Peace Offering   206

Notes & Glossary

FROM

Contrary Visions
(1988)

Contrary Visions in the Gallery, *White on White*

*". . . just a white surface that is simply
a white surface and nothing else."*
    Piero Manzoni

The child in the paisley frock remembers
the terrible storm, how her father saved
her, how suddenly the white winds came.
Stepping forward, she folds her hands
intently into a gesture of peace
like the dove before her, darkening
the surface halfway across the canvas.

Beside her, two mystics vow
this is not the coming of light
or white blossoms at the hands of God,
but a ceremonial stone that brings calm
to any man, if only he will embrace it.

Whereas the artist intended nothing
of this, no more than a white surface,
the lilies I remember turn back years,
and I am a small child again,
comprehending the emptiness of white
offerings, their incantations cold
beside the burial ground. I am moved
by this stillness, by the beguiling white
canvas holding just enough light
to enfold this darkness, this grief.

From the Cloister, Saint Rémy

*"Only when I am working in front
of my easel do I still feel some life . . ."*
        Vincent van Gogh, Saint-Rémy asylum

. . . Their letters and gifts
are treacherous signs.
            When Gauguin sends me
paintings, I struggle with demons.
I hear voices in fields
where wooden crosses twist
heavenward, where precipitous cliffs
rise.
            And Bernard,
who professes to paint
from memory, produces nothing
more than creatures without pain,
saints without bones. I warn you,
Theo, these men deceive us.
Their accusations are wrong. I am not
an abstract painter. You must give them
no support.

            I am weary.
My mind wanders steadily.
Sometimes I see chasms of fire, sometimes
a sky in flames. When the pain enters
my head, it is always the same
undulating motion.
                After a seizure,
they tell me I have kicked
Poulet in the belly, or fallen
beneath barred windows, vials
of turpentine in my hands.

And the one who tries to poison me?
There is something quick
in his eyes. He follows
me through gardens. I know

he is there, a twisted figure
watching me paint. I hear him
whisper: *You are not one of us.*
You are a lowly peasant.
Again and again, the same voice.
                              I must leave
the asylum. I will return
to Holland, to its wheat fields
and rich earth. You must take
me with you, Theo. I will paint
in the open air.

Crows over the Fields of Auvers

*". . . the truth is, we can only
make our pictures speak."*
>Vincent Van Gogh, from a letter found
on his body after his suicide, July 1890,
Auvers

I.
I have been to Auvers
to study the flight of crows
who surely carry pain
in their blood. Today,
feeling the movement
of wheat, they caw a wild
song and with an airiness
that belongs to the wind,
fly low over a patch of earth
in a frenzied dance.

II.
Three is a sacred number.
To this Dutchman, three
meant dirt roads leading
nowhere, crows rising
from horizon toward a space
he chose for death.
He desired light, light
to make his pictures speak.
But unaccustomed to the sun,
he applied violence to the sky,
to the triangular formation
of birds, then stepping back,
with the spirit of a madman
counted to himself
and pulled the trigger.

III.
Now, in the cornfields of Auvers
the air turns warm black
with the progression of crows.
How peaceful, watching
their calm, determined flight
toward the lonely stone.
Cawing as they did years ago,
they call to him one last time
before rising out of golden grasses
and entering a dark blue sky.
All morning the sky deepens,
resuming the unrest below.

Nude Descending in All Directions

After Marcel Duchamp's Nude Descending a Staircase (No. 2), 1912

        Strip her bare.
Swirl her four dimensions
down those stairs stark
naked. She's just another sex cylinder
up your sleeve. Another blown
fuse in your paints.

    You call her revolutionary,
rolling her frame like she's some cause
célèbre?
                      I call her
just another dame gone completely
anti-bourgeois, another one of your
tin lizzies, twitching
her petunia-pink saddlebags.

    She's got *some* high-class itch,
wiggling her dimensions
into anti-art,
into the promised land of Arp
where he who eats Arp eggs
dies, and a single issue of *Rongwrong* prints
her name on a bottle rack
and calls it art.
                      She moves you
into a land where everything's
pataphysics to bruitism,
where blue nudes wiggle their dreams loose,
where Mona Lisa giggles
and exits from the wall
when a readymade coat rack trips
your nude.

    She's balmy, this dame
who shimmy-shakes a wattlebird.

She wiggles out of duck eggs
into Dada.
        Dada's everything coal
black to mousse green.
Dada's *gadji beri bimba glandridi*:
your dame sounding off, popping
rhinoceroses again,
roaring 147
loud times.
    Dada's twittering
bird talk
with a red-breasted goose
like a king of the parallelopipedonists.
        Dada's another chef d'oeuvre
that's hung around forty years,
waiting for an exhibit
on the moon.
            You stripped
your nude bare for this?

The Mathematical Bridge, Cambridge

*A country sky, laced in orange, low-hanging
willows, and a bridge, russet-colored,
move light casually across the River Cam.*

I wake in another country, the absence
of color startling, the room: a lattice
of light and shade, falling

across the wooden floor. Against the wall
stone turrets rise, their silhouettes granite
in a painting where a patchwork of red,

the fabled bridge in the foreground,
links a medieval garden to a brick alcove.
The light settles where the beams interlock,

and I am by the bridge again, by a chapel
where a stained-glass window lifts
blue into a strand, one thin line

crossing the glass the way a thread
rests against embroidered cloth.
I enter the chapel, a woman

who all her life has felt the need
to connect, who reaches out,
lights a candle, the glow entering

the chancel, breaking the coldness
of the evening air. The flame
angles into night, its strength

contained in the way the light lifts
out of darkness. This moment carries me
back to the last time I saw spring

touch the earth, to the place
where country lights brightened,
and I watched an island

of fire, the tips of calla lilies
holding sun, their petals: prisms
separating white into infinite facets.

The complexity, filament by filament,
dims from view where I lie
years later knowing this too

will interlock with time. I look
at the painting, the strength of the bridge
dependent on the strains, each wooden beam

locked in place, the river,
illuminated, still moving this design
through time even as it did years ago.

Touching a Stained-Glass Window in Gloucester Cathedral

For Eddie

Blind boy, I could be particular
and tell you how the design is made,

how faces, folds of drapery
are drawn, then baked in kilns

to flux the paint to the surface.
But how much truer to run

your fingers over colors, to say:
yellow, the imperial crown warms

your palms. Blue, cool fire
of a scepter calms your spirit.

Touch scarlet to understand anger:
not the red of robes that sparkle

with jewels, but flames that angle
and lash through a slate sky.

Feel the power of black where lead
strips give strength to the panes.

Fill your own darkness with soft
winds that rise from the sea, whitecaps

warm as milk lapping your skin.
Let the waves flow to you. Take them

into your heart where everything's
aglow with color and light.

The Aura

*"In the works of man as in those
of nature, it is the intention
which is chiefly worth studying."*
                              Goethe

How intently she guides her brush
hour after hour, the strokes twisting
into flames, some turning crimson,
some sullen against a night sky.
Later, she stands back, stares
at the canvas, not a trace of aura
lifting, the stars random, indistinct.

In the fullness of the design,
she adds hydrangeas to the sky,
blue against half-light, their petals
formed by hands certain of their control.
She lifts darkness into soft winds
before stepping back to study
the hydrangeas, the way they carry light
casually into leaves, how they fold
the air back on a dome of color moving
silence even now into the room.
Look closely. It is the sign
she has waited for, nearly audible,
distinct, and lifting.

What You Hear in a Studio

Sometimes in the middle of a painting
the little things lose control: a stroke
of gray leans into a country barn
like smoke, or one line chases another
along city streets, swerves
left into a fence post
you suddenly put there.

You begin again: this time you imagine
a hawk's cry, ready to paint
his path across the cool green.
A fortunate accident, you whisper
as the sound enters, as moonlight
descends louder through the dark leaves
to surround you in the moment
you listen for.

Forgive Me, But This is Just a Smear of Purple

he says and walks away from my painting,
a young man smug as the cinereous skies

of Long Island where a drab rain falls
and gives seed to nothing. What happens

to him does not matter, I tell myself
admiring the canvas. Picking up a brush,

I enliven the countryside: lavender
fields, cedars, a grove of oak trees

turning orchid as moonlight cloaks
the stars. I wait for a fine,

raking light to clear an opening
in the mist, to pave my way

to the hills where hundreds of stones
hold onto the moon — clean, bleached,

pearly stones that sweep up to greet
the light. Striking a match,

I read my name on a headstone
while the Long Islander chisels

today's date. The blow of steel
against stone wakes me from the vision.

Though it's happened before,
I've come to accept this illusion

as a price to pay for altering
the world so that an ordinary

scene will burn with clarity
and in the palest light, catch fire.

The Peasant Woman above Tarifa

"The shadow is bluest when the body
that casts it has vanished."
                Rafael Alberti

Without warning she appears
in coastal hills, sea winds
blowing, no trees to calm
the land that sweeps like a luminous
shadow under the strait and into
the foothills of another country.

Clearly she has come for flowers,
gathering cluster upon cluster,
her apron swollen, overflowing.
Spanish lace for the children,
she marvels, then loosens
her blouse, uncovering a pendant,
circular, ornate. For a long
time she twirls the necklace
in the sun, and it shimmers.

Light blue, color of mist,
translucent, a Mediterranean moon—
it blues in the eyes of her children
when she returns home, covering
the table with rustling blossoms.

And when she reads to them,
it flutters, a seabird longing
for the slopes above Tarifa,
where it would rinse in the light
this woman left behind, vanishing
into town, her shadow blue,
the earth bluer.

From a Café Window, Tangier

All morning there are suffering women,
a large flaming light, and an artist

sketching figures unaware
of his bold, deft strokes.

You can tell by the way he rocks
their bodies to and fro that the women

are conscious of the sea below.
Stooped over, they are washing

dishes in buckets of water,
the walls of the tenement building

doleful and flat, while the sun
rises toward the center of the sky

and rests. There is no end to what
the artist holds in abeyance,

all trace of human spirit gone,
the sky filled with a false brilliance.

The air grows cold, the stillness
broken by the women disappearing.

From a café window, I watch mist
cover them like a shroud

and in the distance, the artist
barely visible, painting by the sea.

Buttoning my coat to the wind,
I walk the narrow streets for hours

before returning to the studio to add
dark gray to a canvas, a solitary figure

coming into view and before him,
the waves reaching for the shore.

In the Hills of Les Baux

Friends, you did not care
to climb the hills to Les Baux.

So alone, I take in this view:
clear skies to the south

and beneath them Arles,
Saintes-Maries-de-la-Mer.

Here the troubadours found
the source of words, sang

warm nights to women.
Their homes in ruins

glow in the Provence moon
while music pours from stars,

dreamers in love with this city,
its castle walls floating.

Poets, wherever you rest,
sleep in this alluring light

as I will sleep one day,
calmer for having climbed

these hills where the air
taken into the body

feels incandescent and once
released, turns to song.

Spell of Moon and Maple

How is it that the tree
keeps on shining,   *Circling*
its tattered skin   *the tree*
torn by dark mouths   *three times,*
gnawing in a hard wind?

How is it that the tree,   *wander*
worn and alone, reaches   *into a deep,*
into the sky and scatters   *blustery*
October's rubies
over the graying earth?   *night.*

The jewels hold fast
to the bare, flat roots   *Let*
as though feeding hungrily   *the full moon*
on the soul of a tree.   *drop*

Beneath traces of scarlet clouds
fingering the branches,   *from the sky.*
I bend down to gather   *Collect*
pieces of the tree's heart
for my children.

Far from where they sleep,
I rub my fingers over   *the tree's heart.*
the smooth bark.
In the night's stillness
the tree takes the moon   *The children's eyes*

into its arms and spangles   *no longer*
the children's dreams.   *fear the night.*

Baiting My Hook, I Try Again

Just piddling the day away,
my sister says, letting her line
drop to the bottom. I let
my line down, not caring
if the fish bite, figuring
This sure is country living.
Agreeable. Slow. I look back
toward the bridge where storm
clouds gather, and beneath them
rain grays the sky. A sharp
tug on the line, and I reel
in a universe where colors
prevail, where clouds redden
with lightning, a tiny ship fighting
the sea, its bold masts crimson.
Wind rises, and I want
to leave this boat, climb
to the world's roof, paint
dilapidated buildings topaz,
punctuate their pallid shadows.
In this world I want colossal
strings to descend from trees.
Pull one: peaches fall. Another,
plums, dazzling, plump.
I want more strings to fall
from the arms of puppets.
How quickly they gather
baskets for the poor,
parade through India, China,
streets of Africa, hungry
mouths dancing with fruit.
Wine flows into the Ganges, Yangtze,
and Niger, where thousands fill
buckets with the ruby liquid.
Waves slap the boat, and I

climb down from this world.
Reeling in my line, I slide
the worm's frayed skin
from the hook, the fish gone.
This minute the sky opens up.
In my mind, I pull a string
and color the earth for miles
with mulberry light.

Dream: Catching the Air

I.
I watch them lower you.
Each time in the night's
thin hour, you tremble.
Your face, its gaze
once cold under lamplight,
struggles out of a seizure.
You raise your mouth
and breathe back.

Staying long in my dream,
you breathe air
into the mouth laboring
over yours.
Out of a tremor,
you move, catching
air on your tongue
as if you might fill
your lungs.

II.
This morning I place iris
on the bed stand, watch
them turn velvet
as first light floods
your room. Our summers
were like this: opening
windows to mountains,
honeysuckle reaching us
through mist. Afternoons
we wrote on the porch
swing. Always before bed,
you read *Light in August*
or *Les Misérables*.
"What one man won't do

to another," you said resting
your head on the bedpost,
your voice steady.
Now each time you speak
to me in a dream, I wake,
my heart opening, and write
down your words.

III.
For years I go on recording.
This evening shadows
around me flicker, the house
dark. A candle illumines
your picture as a young
girl lying in a bed
of clover. Were you
dreaming, keeping
your mother alive
in sleep? I lean
my head against a chair's
back and doze off.
In a dream you rise
from the clover. Running
toward you, I extend
my arms, taking you in.
Again a seizure pulls
you down. You struggle
for air while moonlight
pours across the floor.
I wake wondering:
How long can we keep
the dead alive this way?
Until the skies darken,
the stars seem to say.
*All these years you have
done it so well.*

The Blind Woman, 1967

I grew old at twenty. The war tugged
at my spirit, Mother drowned in her own fluid,
and I retreated to my room to think of islands

and wildflowers. One evening I wandered
to a grove, climbed sprawling branches,
let the vertiginous wind braid my hair.

I paced in a tree house, latticed with haze,
until my eyes fell on a stranger groping
through darkness, the rap of her cane

audible in the wind. The sidewalk's curve
interrupted her journey. Lost on the lawn,
she tapped the ground for a familiar clink,

this orphaned figure surrounded by stray birds.
Circling through moonlight, she steadied
her stance, the balmy air lowered a shroud,

and I was awed by her struggle.
She struck the sidewalk while shooing
away pigeons, then continued her journey

into the beguiling night. I cannot
forget those eyes, closed as in praise.
I held onto the moon as it found

the spot that had swallowed her.
I wished her farewell, then stepped
back to light, to a field, luminescent.

At the Lawn Party

For Judy, undaunted by her blindness

On the lawn the cooling winds
startle a young woman,
a fine scent alerting her
that someone places a bowl
of fruit on the dinner tray.
It seems a long time
before melons, peaches, berries
warming in the sunlight
touch her lips, the spoon
skimming the surface
lazily, her eyes fragile
stars in the liquid.

Nearby, a man is singing to her.
Poised in her own darkness,
she listens as he defines
honeysuckle, elm, great cedar
trees with a voice that carries
her into a sea of clouds.

I am calmed by a woman who feels
the sweep of my hands as wind
blossoms along her shoulders,
her dignity certain in the way
she knows colors as rainbows.
And all I ask is that
with each spoonful of fruit
she takes into her body,
the rainbows go on
shining as they do now
in the light of her face.

Touch

The boy in the room does not hear
Die Meistersinger, though the rhythm
of the woodwinds touches an old woman
knitting next to him. Her fingers move
deliriously, each loop catching
the air: *Briskness everywhere*,
she marvels, but the child does not
take her words in. Perhaps he is
in an open field where music
as a wind-dance surrounds his body.
He stares so calmly into air's fullness.

The mastersingers take their leave,
but the woman does not notice
the needle lift from the record
or see the late afternoon sun
weave its warmth along her arms.
She is accustomed to darkness,
to the touch of a child's
hand, constant and assured,
wiping the stillness away.

I Don't Know Why I Wake Up Angry

at the young for pushing their mothers
and fathers into nursing homes, for letting
them die hunched over, penniless.

I sometimes walk by asylums repeating
care, care. Lately I have let
the blind keep the lilies I paint,

pounded clay into fists, struggled
to understand the slurred speech
of stroke victims. I have pushed air

into a woman's diseased lungs so she could
praise the prism she held in her hands.
I have run a blind woman's fingers

over Michelangelo's *David* so she would know
he is thinking of enemies, how to escape.
On her death bed, Mother whispered barely

audible strains, echoed this morning
in the rain's breath and years ago
in winds over the burial ground: *Care,*

care, she spoke into a mirror, knowing
the face that stared back would wrinkle
and offend. Last night at Second and D,

I read poetry to the homeless, watched
ladies from St. Elizabeths falter.
Mindless, they drifted toward the fields

portrayed in a poem, pretended to plant
seeds, then knelt in their own bleak
shadows to pray and pray for miracles.

The Visiting Poet, Washington, D.C.

No one below on the expansive lawn,
the streets a maze leading anywhere

this hour of night as you take in
the charm of this city, its marble

and polished granite burning into the sky.
The moon hangs low, every sound lost,

the air motionless where the bridges
cast silver over the river.

You wonder if the spell passes
through other cities—London, Amsterdam,

Rome—whether the wind settles
like light in another place and time.

Musing, you miss a siren's call,
never mind the cries of hookers

and addicts who do not see the moon,
who do not care. And what do you care,

recording the sights of this city?
Tomorrow you will rise to the podium

and recite your poems, drunkards
and bag ladies beyond the Great Hall

humming their songs, their bodies
pressed to the earth among the noble façades.

Gifts

Tonight I bring you Camembert, Brie,
Port Salut, aged to soft yellows
from the hills of France. Delightful,

the way you fold these cheeses into spinach,
how they carry a buttery fragrance
outdoors where children lie, listening

to a wind, bells singing from the steeple
near the corner store. Imagine every evening
like this: counting stars until the sky

becomes a polished lamp. Charmed,
you notice lavender pulled in
from the garden, mounds swelling

to a lavish brown: a roomful of flowers
and breads. Marigolds, violets,
wild plum come to you, the moon.

The sudden smell of wine finds you
dressing flowers, their points
moist with a white as sweet as milk.

A pleasure, the way you fill the distance
with pastures, select the blackest cows
for cream. This is more than imagination:

the aroma of bread rising
about the kitchen, the Brie's
smooth skin gently darkening.

FROM

Gathering Light
(1993)

As a Teacher I'm Inclined to Ignore the Critics

who say Georgia O'Keeffe's flowers are female
parts, her Lawrence tree a monstrous phallus,

who failed themselves as artists. I'm apt
to let my class loose in O'Keeffe's heroic

light so they can soak in the spirit of a private
mountain painted so many times she ought to have

owned it. I'm prone to let the children search
the red hills and bones for a mystery, let them create

a movie script about *Horse's Skull with White Rose*:
a cowgirl, for example, three months dead in the desert,

nothing left but calcified bones, a lover's parched rose
fastened to the horse's forehead. Which myopic

critic said, *There is nothing here but confusion
on a large scale*? I tell my students to lie close

to her shells and listen to the wind sing in marble
shadows, to carry that music in their heads so they too

can fashion a world as though they're the first to see it:
lone tree in the full sky and this feeling of grand space.

Red Poppy

*"Still – in a way – nobody sees a flower – really –
it is so small – we haven't time – and to see
takes time, like to have a friend takes time."*
                    Georgia O'Keeffe

To see the flower,
            to really see it
takes time: knowing
            what to praise
and for how long. Suppose
            the poppy's a scarlet
ibis afloat on a bed
            of leaves, cardinals
in flight, a tanager calling
            its mate. The artist
enlivened this flower
            so you could know it.
Yet here you stand
            befuddled by a poppy:
recognizable, small,
            delicate as a robin.
Relax. Try not to stare
            so hard. It knows
you're here admiring
            its birdlike petals.
Opalescent, the red
            poppy shines from within,
dark, oval center
            clipped from a swath
of velvet cloth.
            You can feel the wings
sway: five of them
            on a huge scale
gathering sun.
            Not one of us
can ignore their
            willful beauty.

Above Clouds

From an airplane Georgia O'Keeffe changed the world
into a Z waving its curvaceous tail, an *altiplano*
of clouds, ridges, water holes, the brown pattern

of the Amarillo country. *Fly higher*, the winds called.
So in Abiquiu she began sleeping on the roof
where she dreamed of the odd dark and the bright

look that overtook her each morning when she walked
out of shadows and saw the long mesa line, moon
above it, curve of a low wall, Red Hills out beyond

the wide valley as if across water. She walked
through the lifting sun over purple earth
to pick *chimaja* which sweetened her hands

while she colored a canvas with small fragrant leaves.
At night she brightened the sky over her patio;
the moon sanctified a cache of white bones.

She gave us white, anointed by red or black,
to show her love for shells and skulls.
She painted a single poppy, a calla lily, her ranch

door. To her it was breathtaking to simplify
the wind, dust, the vast blue. Through an open
window, all the cottonwood trees, the wide stretch

along the river valley, the unchanging Pedernal
moved right into her studio as a jack-in-the-pulpit
erupted out of her smooth ethereal colors.

Beneath Lamplight

Who can say why the old Dutch painters
ignored the diggers of earth, assiduous
toilers seated by huts washing

turnips and beets? Today I labor
in the field, my reward: plump
potatoes resplendent in the soil's

dark shine. I make a meal of the fleshy
vegetable as I believe Vincent did
after painting *The Potato Eaters,*

thus blessing the common meal
his peasants chose, gathered
around a table in lamplight.

Reaching for the platter, I let
myself become one of his Dutch women,
gnarled hands browned as if pulled

from loam. I roam vast stretches
of land where furrows absorb
evening's glow. Walking with peasants

bearing the last bundles home,
I feel comfort in my new calloused
skin. The workers empty their sacks,

mounds striking the table. They sit
down in darkness and find extraordinary
light in each other's eyes.

In Rodin's Studio at Meudon

I would like to have studied Rodin
at work: women in constant
motion, one supple as she
twirls a ribbon,
another

gathering her golden hair, swiveling
just as the master, quick
as a child, seizes
clay and enlivens
the pose.

He has the hands of a pianist, fingers
in flight, taut as they shape her
muscular limbs. How long
must he hold these
hands

close to his work before a figure
curls into song, the curve
of a spine creased
with shadows
advancing

the body's length? The models swirl
and twist past Rodin until they
rest in space like
marionettes
without

strings. One of the women stirs,
lifts her arms and captures
the secret of dance:
her legs, fully
awake,

as movement mounts her frame, ribs
extended, eyes warming the sky.
Rodin turns his back,
selects an older
model

who lowers her head, light illuminating
the gray hair, sagging breasts,
all the delicate shapes.
Lost in thought,
she slips

one hand behind her, the other planted
on a rock, neck and back straining
with age. Rodin fashions her
veins so blood can
pulse freely,

rounds the stomach, captures her
breathing. He knows her body
can be beautiful: this
courtesan who casts
her eyes

down as if suffering. I would like
to have witnessed the heightening
of dignity: the old
woman seated in
a vaporous

glow, heavy shadows folding into flesh
so finely wrought by the master
that her divine body
dissolves all sense
of time.

Father

There's no need to fear death,
my father told me when I was four,

his arms holding me above the casket
where my grandmother lay asleep:

just that, asleep, he said
so convincingly I believed him

then and when he died, gripping
my hand as if to take me

where time doesn't matter,
where, as he said, I'd ride a horse

over cloud beds, rise beyond cerulean
sky into a void which he promised me

is not empty, but full of children's
stories, my twenty cats, giant

maples to climb, and as he told
me this, I looked into his eyes

and felt his abundant spirit
that would stop my watch

the moment he died, his spirit
that would set off the smoke alarm

in his house the hour he was cremated,
his spirit that would continue

its flight into a void, gathering
light, while ribbons of sun

lifted him from the deathbed
as I gazed upon his sleeping face.

The Hibiscus

On the anniversary of my father's death, July 12, 1993

Twelve straight days of this hot spell,
the roses, flat red, broken-down beauties,
morning just up, warming itself.

A week, I have waited for the hibiscus
to flower, wondering its color and whether
all this heat has kept it from opening —

when suddenly, there it is: red
blossom of your heart beating,
a sign like rain letting down a veil

of berries, the *plink, plink* as rhythmic
as your words; or the sun, orange giant,
waiting for me near the horizon;

or cypress, sun-glazed steeple, standing
straight up, as you said I should do
whenever sorrow, overabundant, hurt me.

O, my father, I could grieve, but a breeze
says don't, and heat clings to me
like honey, the moisture on my skin lemon-

silk, and the voices of birds, bursts
of yellow, spun, spun through heavy air.
In my palms, I cradle your heart,

a blessing. At night when this piece
of you falls off its branch, I will
place it in a chalice of water

and wait for the hibiscus to flower
again. O, Father, for me summer has
always been these blooms, these blooms!

You Don't Need Binoculars to be a Bird Watcher

Take Lake Nakuru in Kenya, the vast number
of flamingos. What greater bird than the Lesser:
carmine-red, the legs startle the water.

Perched on stilts, it slips
its bill beneath the surface, flips
its tongue into place, then dips

for algae. Outnumbered, the Greater towers
to six feet, feeds on mollusks, then clears
the lake, soars over tiers

of yellow acacias glinting in pure
sun. Rock-strewn hills, every detour
opens up on pelicans, seems an overture

to the view at the top: pink slides from sky
like a rainbow into your eyes
mesmerized by the flight. You ask why

there are so many birds rushing
to earth. Don't waste time looking
through binoculars. Start running

to the lake's edge for a closer view.
Look into the liquid heart where the blue-
green pulsates, red beaks sucking, then spew-

ing out water. Follow the pelicans' snow-white
ascent into the flamingos' flight.
Be like the birds. Lift. Ignite.

Balloon Safari over Masai Mara

After a champagne breakfast we crawl into the stomach
of a round bird that lifts straight up. The flames
subside as the balloon catches a wind so fanciful

we glide along as if pulled by invisible filaments.
At these heights the world becomes a playground
of toy animals. A giraffe, galloping over grassland,

dwindles to a size a child can raise to the tops
of acacia trees. A cape buffalo, brave fighter
snorting a challenge to another bull, courts

a charitable egret on his bantam back. In a Lilliputian
state, lions feed on dwarfish wildebeest and zebra.
Humans beside me do not shrink in this whimsical world.

A fellow traveler, blind to my vision, points to the sun
tinting earth orange. I am too absorbed in my kingdom
and this newfound bravery to care about the sunrise.

Reaching down, I pick up the champion runner, its spotted
body no larger than my index finger. I let the sleek
cheetah go, watch its attack on a herd of gazelles.

Approaching the Mara River, I sweep up a handful
of hippos, plump hairless river horses searching for grass
in the creases of my palm. Releasing them in water,

I lean forward, unscathed, as a male rends another.
A black rhino, horns so tiny they barely pierce
the skin, tears out of my grasp and jolts me awake.

My companions snap pictures of a lioness stalking
through golden grass while I, a proud huntress, zoom in
on the savanna swelling to its legendary size.

When Birds Speak

*"To Shakespeare, they were not isolated objects
but living creatures."*
    Levi Fox, *Shakespeare's Birds*

How can one ignore his chattering pies,
a lapwing close to earth, every goose
cackling, a strutting chanticleer?
They are all there in his drama:
dive dapper, pigeon, woodcock, wagtail—
and among them, such pretty talk.
Did he study birds to see how all
creatures work, how man in his folly
climbs commanding peaks? A vulture
circles, then swoops. In the shadow
of its wings, wren and robin hover
over their young. They are all there.
Swift flight: the swallow points
its wings and ascends while thrush
and jay harmonize with wind.
And the graceful swan, what metaphors
did he see in her: royal birth, music,
majestic curves of the universe?
He must have sat next to her,
away from paper and ink, with her
neck arced like a river's bend.
He must have seen prisms in those
feathers, prisms in expanded wings.
When the birds spoke the language
of waves, they flew to him out of elm
and ash. Always a triumph: birds
on every branch and the playwright
in his haven learning to sing.

The Rosetta Stone

*Vulture, flowering reed, wick of twisted flax,
quail chick.* I scan the list of hieroglyphic
signs, pictured and labeled in a museum
guidebook, then search the Rosetta Stone
for *Ptolemy* and *Cleopatra* locked in the basalt
slab found two centuries ago in Rashid.
Gazing at elongated signs, I think of you,
miles between us dissolving, your forefinger
whirling to shape *el remolino,* the Spanish accent
thick as you say whirlwind in English.
Graceful, the long-stemmed *clavel* you hold up
to the light to say carnation, not *roja*
but *rosado,* the color of roses blooming
in your floral shirt. Bleating like a goat,
you carry me to the Andes where we drink
la leche de las cabras, the liquid warming
our limbs, a comfort on wind-swept slopes.
And so we learn each other's language, drawing
pictures in midair or cawing the crow's talk.
So simple compared to these hieroglyphics
where men let the head subjugate the heart
to decipher the stone's mysteries. Why not
this way: a scholar enjoys a good wine
before bed, falls into a deep sleep, dreams
of stars over the Western Delta, demotic
and Greek falling into patterns his waking
mind can't see. I search the stone for emotion
among the scripts, think of our translations
disappearing in air as soon as we shape
a cross or mew a cat's cry. The heart's
the key: letting the mind go so the spirit
can fly wildly about the room, lifting
the window and reaching sky.

Something of Myself

I awake to rain. Listening
to the cadence takes me back
to a country where there is no rain

in winter, sun anointing Peruvian
fields, patches of corn glistening.
In the Sacred Valley I find

something of myself in Incas
shouldering bundles of sticks,
their bare feet calloused by land,

at 10,000 feet, something of myself
in Indians tilling slopes, and proud.
They tell me I am a stranger

because I was not born here.
Though I speak little Quechua,
I am no stranger to flute

calls and dancers — their rhythms
lured me as a child, our house
alive with *El Condor Pasa*.

Far from the coastland, I find
my childhood suspended in the blend
of rock and violet peaks, in eucalyptus

leaves, in lingering Scotch Broom:
images set loose each time I read
Neruda's *Alturas de Macchu Picchu*.

There is something of home
in climbing these sculpted terraces.
At the top, I scoop up a handful

of soil, taste its grain,
its warmth feeding my hunger
for the hillsides of western

Virginia where as a child
I planted corn and potatoes.
Though at home there is no

southern sky, each night stars
spill their legends, and in all
that brightness, who can tell

north from south? In Pisac,
in Ollantaytambo, in Machu Picchu,
I hear the bell-call of rain.

Among the Ruins of Puca Pucara, Perú

All afternoon she follows us
around the grounds of Puca Pucara,
the shepherdess who dances

when I give her a fountain pen
for school. A gracious present,
the young girl's smile, her alpacas

grazing on tufts of *ichu* grass.
Where she wanders, the red fortress
glistens. Stone terraces brighten

her wavering shadow. Blue, the color
of air so pure in these mountains
that silver does not tarnish.

Nor do the reds, yellows, greens
of her gathered skirt lose
their shine in the azure light.

I want to remember this child
scurrying over slopes, her
bare feet soiled with dust.

I want to remember her *Por favor,
señorita*—as she begged
for my pen. She has been schooled

well in the craft of panhandling,
a child who now gazes
at her mother for approval.

Machu Picchu

*Rediscovered by Hiram Bingham in 1911, this lost Inca city lies
8000 feet above sea level in the Andes of Perú.*

Nothing as predictable as this narrow gauge train
   chugging each day from Ollantaytambo past barley,
     olluco, quinoa fields through a granite gorge
        to this station in the jungle where thick undergrowth
          hides terraces that have endured for centuries.

A mantle of light hovers over bananas, wild
   papaya, the train slowing at Puente Ruinas.
     Climb, the Andes say to me. *Climb and witness my
       miracles. Others before you have touched these peaks,
         taken them back to countries where mountains can never

rival what is mine. What is yours, I answer, *is
   the need to rise miles above the sea, to charm
     at these heights with masks of greenery, to deceive
       with fortresses built upon your shoulders, to cover
         yourself with a golden fragrance: Scotch Broom dotting*

garments of field and stone. Up an ancient pathway,
   across one strip of road, across another, I climb,
     never doubting the city at the top. My feet covered
       with dust, I channel energy into the body's
         center, free my mind, and visualize the way up.

At the top who can say this is less than the world's
   finest painting? Clouds more precise than a Constable
     landscape, their billowy composition hangs in
       abeyance. Towering mountains, layered as if caught
         in a whirlwind, encircle this peak. Stones, chiseled

and carried down from a quarry, shape these houses
   that earthquakes have not felled. And the spirit
     of the ruins is so pure all races, cultures, the rich,
       the poor, all who climb to this pinnacle are equal.
         The midday sun close to earth showers the Andes.

I glance down on the Rio Urubamba winding
    its way through the Sacred Valley, its rapids and falls
        furious as crazed lions, Machu Picchu a bird
           on its perch, its wings tucked in, a bird safe above
                the canyon, safe for decades under wild growth, no

conquistador clever enough to find Machu Picchu.
    Through temples, palaces, I walk through the sky's sanctum
        searching for the chosen women of the sun.
           By the houses of the guardians, by the funerary
                table: orchids, begonias, lilacs bloom. It is spring

in the city of the skies. And when it is spring,
    the sun shines so intensely that at this altitude
        the flow of its energy rushes through the body,
           the sun that fed the Incas' llamas and alpacas,
                the sun that shone on Intihuatana, its prism

raised over natural stone. Reaching the sundial at noon,
    a traveler pulls crystals from his pocket to energize.
        I expand my chest and breathe deeply, the oxygen
           thin, my head faint from the flow of sensations I do
                not want to lose: the sky an impenetrable blue,

the traveler peaceful, crowds around him drawing nearer.
    How could the Incas have known the secret of stone?
        They chiseled one to fit another, then lifted
           each stone into place. From the sundial the ruins shine
                like emeralds, clouds and mist cleanse the walls, sharpen

the parrot-green of terraces. How many other
    cities lie hidden in this jungle? I turn toward
        the canyon, see archaeologists uncovering
           a trail, the terraces barely visible. They will find
                other cities. I stand in the making of history

embracing these Andes, their fertile peaks solid
    and full of stories children ought to hear. At these heights,
        everyone finds a segment of the soul. Returning
           home has always seemed faster than traveling to new
                lands. But today, leaving will be a long journey.

Christmas in Bolivia

On the streets of Cochabamba, Indian women sell miniatures of Mary, Joseph, the three kings. My husband holds up a four-foot pine, bargains the price down, then smiles, boyhood all over his face, good to be home where he can decorate the tree in the native reds, greens, and blues of this fertile pampa. Hot, the streets of this city, close to the sun. I look up at the fabled god *Inti* showering the cathedral, its tower of bells and clock marking the hour: noon, the stone condor aloft its perch in the plaza *Catorce de Septiembre*, mythical bird lifting its wings brought alive by *Inti's* fire and the trick of midday glare.

My husband drops *bolivianos* into the cup of a blind woman seated by the cathedral doors. Her face, furrowed and browned, softens in the protective shadows as if she senses the sparrow skittering toward her. Flapping its wings, it lifts, then touches down on the woman's cup, tipping it over, causing her to jump and grab the tin vessel as if to avoid a robber. My husband leans down and rights the container. Speaking in soothing tones, he pours the coins from the cup into her hands so she can count them, their size and weight familiar to her fingers.

I lower my head and ask for the sparrow to bless this Indian woman. In the square someone plays the *quena* as though he has swallowed the wind.

Mariano Quispe

Mariano Quispe can recite by heart the Inca emperors from Pachacuti to Atahuallpa. A keeper of history, he spins alpaca wool into yarn, the strings turning the color of honey or topaz as if woven by a sun god.

This morning he knots strings that coil into hemp beads, one strand crossing itself once, another three times before the maker's eyes fill with satisfaction. As the sun peaks over the Andes, Mariano pauses in prayer because he loves the way his strings sing in the rising light. To him, they are turquoise of dawn, golden cornfield, jungle sapphire, emerald rapids.

His leathery hands preserve what the men of Micaypata want to remember, the knots on one string increasing to eight, numbering his neighbor's alpacas, more wool for the winter nights. He twists an amber string, then shapes twenty knots to count baskets of corn. When Mariano finishes, he stores the *quipu* with the others in a large weathered jar, the elaborate necklaces holding onto the recent history of the hamlet, all ancestral records lost when the conquistadors burned the storehouse of *quipus*.

At noon Mariano rests, his strings forgotten. He does not think about the person who, years later, will try to decode his colorful knots. He has worked hard this morning, and now he must offer thanks to *Inti* for his *chicha* and bread.

In a Field by Lake Titicaca

I.
As a girl, I played the part of Indian
princess, each arm costumed in glittering
bracelets that became real with the wave
of my hand. Beside me on a moss-throne
sat my imaginary prince proud as a lofty oak,
and American: Cherokee, Maya or Inca,
never mind the continent. Years later
I married my Indian, strong Quechua blood,
tongue of the Incas, Protector of Animals.
Sheep, llamas, birds flock to him.

II.
Today in Huatajata, a cold wind cuts
across Lake Titicaca, a crouched puma
against the *altiplano*. By the lake's edge
a lamb, still young enough to nurse, cries
for its mother, its foreleg tangled in a rope
secured to a post. My husband stoops,
loosens, unties until the bleating stops.
The animal searches our palms for food.
Feeling the give of the rope, he scampers
off leaving us free to continue our walk
by the lake, beryl blue in full sun.

III.
I came here to see the soil my husband
tilled as a boy planting *papas*, tubers worth
more than silver to hungry mouths. I imagine
he waved his hand over the land to enrich
the soil, the ground swelling with potatoes.
I imagine the fields turned yellow and orange
as they do now under his touch in the rarefied
air. I watch him walk through a field
of quinoa flowing like the waters. The wind
ripples his shirt as he feeds a llama,
one hand full of ripening grain, the other
stroking the long, fleeced neck.

IV.
Clouds gather and move across the lake
like swallows. From a grove of trees
the notes of a *quena* rise, the history
of these highlands streaming into the field
where my husband looks for the elusive
condor. He calls to me, Bolivian folklore
of his past coming alive in this world
two and a half miles above sea. My head
reeling, I hurry into the field, recalling
those days on a moss-throne. I wave
my hands and fill the sky with condors.
My husband swings me into air
as if the birds are really there.

FROM

Death Comes Riding
(1999)

The Healing

In sleep I saw the muddy water
covering my feet and rising.
A sign of illness, my mother warned,
and in dream after dream
the turbulent waters deepened.
When I fell ill that sultry summer
thirty years back, the marigolds
lost their scent and withered.
Near-death came, and I rose
into a cream-colored sky, hovered
over the bed, the room airless.
The miracle came in an old-fashioned
courtesy call from the family doctor,
life being simple and honest.
Always, my luck has startled me.
This morning, for example, the cat,
sensing sadness, jumps into my lap
and kneads his paws so I will
praise him. *A little gift,* my mother
called it whenever the habitual turned
wondrous. I pat the cat's sleek fur,
the purring so close to what I am feeling,
his lick cleansing my forearm
and in the distance, the doctor's
careful hold as he lifts me from the bed.

The Telephone Ring

It used to be like this at 11:30 p.m.: gutsy,
terse, a half-ring, then an echo that droned on.

My husband heard it too, the impetuous
b-r-r-i-ng. I was afraid at first, but rational

thought eased me. *Some pervert's calling
for a thrill,* I quipped. I nervously

laughed at each night's maddening ring.
Ordered another phone to prove

that one bad. Snuffed out the crooked
sound with a faithful prayer.

*

I wonder if it's my mother calling.
As a child when I wrestled with sky

demons who threw me from half-sleep
into the murky seas, she rescued me.

In her arms I could touch distant harbor
lights. In her arms seas silvered into the grit

of day. Years later, in a swirling pool
of lung fluid, she drowned at 11:30 p.m.

*

I no longer listen for the ring, though
late nights it's there, a cadence.

When my husband comes to bed, I think
about the two of us, yet twenty

or thirty years from death, pondering
a sound that's come to mean something.

What if it rings for those who pray to the dead?
For me, it's their way to keep us near.

Mother

I fear night
    until I find
        moon.
After dark, she scoops me
    up into her
        brightness
where I wander
    among spirits
        let loose
from the heavens: my mother,
    thirty years
        dead,
visits me often.
    Sometimes I see her
        running free
through luminous fields.
    Once from a cloud's
        savannah
she tamed a thunderbolt's
    whiplike snap
        at my feet.
Tonight moon dips
    into *Sagrada Familia,*
        Notre Dame,
into all of the world's churches.
    Mother alights in the sanctum
        of my heart.
Here, she teaches me
    about stone's durability,
        what it means
to outlast illness,
    how to take
        the years
I've been given and to fling
    them into air

                    so they multiply,
so they ring through darkness.
          I gather up
                    her words,
then retreat to my study.
          In the picture of us
                    on the wall,
I am a child, kneeling
          at her feet,
                    listening.

Katherine Anne Porter's Secret

Come into the library, he said, *and I will show you Katherine Anne's secret.* Among the rare
books the coffin stood on end, six feet of pine

painted Mexican style. I'll never forget
the decorative reds that rose to greet us.
Staring at the private box, I imagined her

lighting one last lamp before stepping in,
those violet eyes alert, her white hair
turning black in burial flames.

*When I die, I will have the coffin
and linen sheet ready,* she told a friend
one February, the plate-glass windows

of her apartment rattled by wind, her voice
shrill, determined. I watched the pine box
change into a ship headed from Veracruz

to Bremerhaven. She curled within it,
searching for a sign. *May I stand in it*?
I asked, touching the coffin.

My friend ran his fingers over
the long brass hinges, opened the lid.
Unafraid, I stepped in. My mind raced

back fourteen years to a room filled
with caskets where Father and I selected
a blue one for Mother. I realized then

that death can hold us for only a second
before disappearing, Mother's spirit
having risen out of my dream the night

she died. *We control our souls*, she said
once, rocking on the porch swing.
For years I held onto her words.

I pressed my body against the coffin's
walls, hoping to leave an impression full
of flight like the snow angels I had made

as a child. The afternoon filtered in,
my eyes refocusing on brass fittings
and plain wood. I stepped back into

the room, rested my hand on the smooth
lid, closed it gently. Katherine Anne died
the next month. That night at home, I lit all

the lamps, rose the next morning to find only
one still burning. As I leaned down to turn
it off, my eyes caught in the mirror a figure

draped in Liège linen. The face warmed
the darkness, then vanished. All morning
I read her stories in strong daylight.

All Saints' Day

*"I want to sleep a while, . . . a minute, a century;
but let everyone know that I am not dead."*
                    Federico García Lorca

When I was eight, no one believed there were ghosts
in our house, except a close friend who heard them

turn on the upstairs faucet once, the air chilled
when we arrived in time to catch them disappearing

through the hallway's blanched walls. Truth is
they were there all along. I heard their heels

tapping the floorboards. At night they slithered
beneath my bed, terrified me until Mother cradled

my head so I could doze off, phantoms, demons,
ghouls, wickedness vanishing in her presence.

        *

At sixteen I nearly became a ghost,
illness squeezing the will and drive out of me.

That night I floated above myself into a lucid sky,
the fear of dying gone so that over the years

I have come to respect ghosts, their unexpected
appearance, the need to suspend belief

in order to feel their presence. I suppose
you might say I'm good at it after all this time.

        *

Recently in Bolivia on All Saints' Day, my basket
overflowed with sacks of flour, candy, fruit

and drink for the spirits of the dead. My husband
and I had just returned from market, our deceased

relatives about to visit. We prepared beans in hot
sauce, egg biscuits, *chicha morada*, a rich corn drink.

Legend says the dead protect us if we take care
of them. To highland Indians, this means strong rains

for crops. We lined a table with bread-baked llamas,
sheep and birds to carry souls back from far-off lands.

At noon, church bells rang the arrival of the souls.
My husband and I ate enough for two, knowing

that whatever we consumed would, by faith, satisfy
the dead. The next day we set a small feast

on cemetery graves. *Resiris*, supplicants, prayed
for the dead while we bid farewell to our relatives.

*

Back home, I mull over Lorca's words, mull over
how not to die, how to leave something behind:

a sculpture, a well-taught child. Mull over
if the highland Indians have it right: that after we die

our souls climb out of the prayers of descendants,
bowed over our graves, so they can release us

from death once a year to wander earth and revere it
the way we should have when we were alive.

Fifth Wife, Hampton Court Palace

*Henry VIII's wife, Catherine Howard, was accused
of committing adultery with Thomas Culpepper,
a young man of the court. She was beheaded
for this indiscretion on February 13, 1542.*

          I shall never make love to him again,
Thomas. Those corpulent jowls. Why, the man's
smitten with dropsy.
                        And the servants?
Gossips. In every corner of the palace, vigilant.
But let's not heed them. While Henry's up north,
we have Hampton Court.
                            Come forth
to the gardens. I long for the delirium of roses,
for the mild-mannered Thames. A stroll shall ease
our minds. The King does not control
us. Nor does this monstrous place, its clocks, bells,
guards, the ladies-in-waiting.
                            I sometimes think
death consumes these halls. It crawls on the brink
of madness when Henry calls me to his bed.
That ulcerous man, I detest his obesity spread
over me like a shield.
                But I must let go of these thoughts
and distance myself from displeasure. Caught
as we are in this tangle, let us be off.
                                  There,
already I feel the fullness of sun, the air
swollen with the willful chirping of wrens
and swallows.
                You recall my cousin, Anne Boleyn,
who cherished birds? Downcast as she was,
they bolstered her spirits. A pity, she fussed
with the King, her savage tongue breaking the spell,
and that callous man getting rid of her, all
out of greed for another woman.
                            I do worry
he will find out about us, Thomas, but he dotes on me,
and I, forgiving myself, will crawl to his chamber,
flatter, appease him until his coffers stir.

Vigil

*In 1858 John Gray's loyal dog followed its master's
remains to Greyfriars Kirkyard, Edinburgh, and lingered
near the gravesite until its death in 1872.*

Faithful friend, you stood watch over my grave.
Crouched beneath a tablestone, you braved

sleet and snow. Not even the kirkyard spectres
frightened you from this vigil. Sometimes here

where you lay, the ground encircled me with warmth,
and I remembered you trotting to market along a footpath.

Seller-women, laden with goods, tossed a half-penny's
worth of bread to the Constable's watchdog, the shaggy

fur that covered your eyes, a beggar's gift. Nights,
rain-swept, we rounded the cemetery in the deadlight.

To fight the chill, you must have dreamed
of the banks of whin, of wild rabbits chased

out of lairs across fields, belled with blue blossoms.
When I fell ill, you lingered nearby, never strayed from

my heart; even as I died, wee terrier, you bequeathed
your loyalty, followed my coffin to this patch of earth.

For fourteen years you roamed the Old Town streets.
The people loved you. Some gave you milk, fed you meat

leftover from a tavern's fare. Each nightfall
you returned to me until one Sunday, vesperal

chants rose in wintry air. Some say a dog's spirit yields
to dust, but I see you running in the sky fields.

The Anne Frank House at Prinsengracht 263

Neither the dutiful walls, nor worn-out bookcase meant
      to unlock the house's secret, nor the stately tree
in the courtyard, its graceful limbs outstretched like angels.

    Anne longed for a solitary space
              in the house.

Unrelenting, the sun betrayed the inhabitants. Searching,
      it poured through windows, asked if any Jews
lived here. That summer the house knew its fate.

    She longed for her own window
              and the clear light.

A parked lorry, the Nazis pounded
      on the door. An informant among them
pointed toward the bookcase.

    No opaque curtains to muffle her
              beloved church chimes.

When they opened the back annex, the Prinsengracht
      flowed freely, and gulls, well-fed, filled
the abundant branches. With a high-pitched shrill,
      they drowned out the victims' cries.

    In privacy, she could lose herself
              in dreams.

Its secret told has been a burden on the stairs,
      floors, the rooms behind the hinged bookcase.
When workers restore the house, they must not
      change the dim light, the scratches on walls.

    All alone, she turned words
              into flight.

Leaving a Country Behind

I.
Rain over Munich, your plane's
clothed in a monk's black.
You look around the cabin
and wonder how the people
go on sleeping, rumors
over the radio of death
and hunger. Staring
into darkness, you see
your aunt cupping a fresh
bouquet, saying goodbye
to a stranger, someone
who knew about Dachau,
how long it takes to burn
the eyes shut. Again
there is lightning
and the murmur of her voice.
Father, how many times
must you leave a country
where the eyes praise nothing?

II.
I will always remember
the way your aunt said *Hitler*,
her lips drawn into a hiss
and then freed. Loving words,
I repeated *Hit* with a lilt
and then *ler*, too young
to understand the history
one man left behind
buried in this woman's heart.
I remember drawings hung
about the house, the time
she locked herself in the attic
to sketch a mad giant.
At the funeral, you placed
a rose in her lap.
The choirboy sang as if
the past were but a moment
he could bury with the dead.

III.
Drive twelve miles northwest,
the villager said, pointing
the way to the death camp.
I was six years old,
and today my mind returns
to Dachau, to the barbed
wire, ovens, and wooden bunks,
to iron bodies writhing
in a sculpture displayed
for the world's children.
Father, even now as the rains
fall, I hear sounds rising
from the dead and somewhere
beyond the rain, the voice
of a German offering her rose.

Ice Maiden

In 1995, anthropologist, Dr. Johan Reinhard, discovered in Peru a 500-year-old mummy sacrificed to the sacred mountain, Ampato.

I.
I did not want to return to my body,
one hand caught in a death grip,
my own skin leathery, teeth bared—
all of me in frozen ruins.
When they found me, a mummy cast
out on a field of snow, they called
me regal: rhapsody of raven hair,
neck arced, cheekbones raised
toward the spirit world. I came
back to the flesh once I heard
a voice calling from the mountain's
surface, my grave torn open,
my body exposed. I had to protect
the burial grounds.

II.
Far from home, I tell myself
it is only for a while that I must
remain a prisoner in this artificial
tomb of ice. Sometimes I feel
lightning in my heart. I scream
in a thunderous voice, but no one
hears me through these glass walls.
If they freed me, I would tell them
how I became Ampato's gift.
A maiden, I was carried to the peak
like a sacrificial llama.
I begged the mountain deity
to drench the parched earth.
How proud Mama and Papa were
that I was chosen. They fed me
chicha, corn beer, before I died.

My parents had labored over it
in my honor. The priest offered
the mountain coca leaves, gave me
some to chew to dull the senses
so I would not feel the sharp blow
of death, only the comfort of Ampato's
arms as he drew me close.

III.
I do not belong in this strange body.
I belong in the center of the mountain,
in the spirit world where I can
take care of my people. I long for
the snow's warm mantle, for the wind's
weight pushing me deep into the whiteness
where a river can flow out of itself,
rain down on my descendants' fields
and feed the hungry soil.

Elena Mesa

In 1931 shortly after 22-year-old Elena Mesa
died of tuberculosis, her doctor exhumed her
body and lived with the mummified remains
in a hideaway in Key West, Florida.

Señor von Cosel, you were never my lover,
though you forced me to lie with you,
breathed air into my hardened lungs, covered
my bones with spun silk, pursued
me. May Holy Mary undo your sin.
The night you took me from the tomb
I saw myself in the stars, skin
pocked and hollowed, my hair's bloom
gone, my voice echoing, but no one there.
Did you, sick with love, think you could bring life
back with netting and wax, repair
my hands and feet, make me your wife?
Unholy man, I'm stunned by your disgrace.
Erase these years. Give me back my resting place.

The Sacred Valley

I have learned how to breathe
in this valley. Here the glimpse

of a condor leads me into flight.
I am told if I pray, a deity

will carry me to the Andes' heights.
Today it is enough to stand

beneath peaks. Clouds waver
like snowcaps ready to melt,

and once melted, rush into valleys
to nourish soil for *campesinos*

who bow down to the *cordillera*
for sending headwaters and rain.

Grain strapped to their backs,
llamas stop on riverbanks to drink.

I listen to the delicate lapping.
I will learn the language of this place.

The Quechuan Boy of Cuzco

Each night the Quechuan boy sold pottery outside our door. The chill did not seem to bother him, a thin sweater his only guard against the cold.

One morning on the way to Chinchero, we spotted him scampering down a slope toward an adobe hut, purple fields of amaranth lining the hillside. He knelt and gave a basket of corn to his mother, weaving an orange rug, chickens and guinea pigs scurrying about the courtyard. No one saw us come or go, our bus out of place in the rugged highlands. A eucalyptus grove swallowed us as we rounded a curve.

We saw him again in Plaza de Armas, the giant bell of Maria Angola pealing from the cathedral's north tower, celebrating our chance meeting. He chatted about his family's patches of land. Refusing money, he gave us each a small earthen pot, then started the long walk home.

The last day he peered through the bus door, our leaving marked by the smell of *anticuchos*, the haunting notes of a *toyo* pouring from a restaurant's open window. I snapped his picture as he handed my friend a farewell gift. When the bus pulled off, I put the camera down, the boy running behind us. Alongside the road the rippling eucalyptus trees called us back.

Azucena's Arpillera

When I was five, I stitched my first *arpillera*. The next morning I showed my mother what I had sewn: fields bursting with potatoes and lettuce the size of clay bowls. She laughed and said, "But, Azucena, you need a river as wide as sky, the great Andes and sun to bless your vegetables!"

That night after a meal of *chicharrón*, Papa blew powerful notes from the *zampoña*, notes that swayed through fields of *maíz* in a fanciful dance. The music collected starlight that fell like silver over the crops. Our neighbor by the fire passed down folklore to his children. In the distance a *quena* whistled.

The moon curved like a *pututu* and descended from the top of the sky when the night angel appeared astride a llama. Never before had I seen a wrap as magnificent as hers, red, orange, blue, green singing against the snow of her llama. Without dismounting, she unfolded the shawl: berries crimson, magenta root, blue dust falling in streams so plentiful I could scarcely contain them in the basket of my skirt. "The secret is the color," she whispered, then vanished into perfumed air.

I took the treasure, ground berries, root, dust into magical dyes that turned woolen cloth into grass of the valley, into the Andes bronze, into water turquoise and flowing. When I had finished, I showed my parents the *arpillera*, its alpacas grazing on *ichu* grass. The way they touched the cloth, I knew they saw themselves plowing fields and baking bread. I wondered if the night angel had appeared to them.

The Inca Dolls

I saw them first in a shop window in Cuzco, then later in the soiled palms of an Indian child whose eyes held the past of the Inca dolls I bought because their clothing smelled like warm Andean dirt. I was told the child's mother made them from an ancestor's garments, perhaps one who had kneeled in a field to dig potatoes for her family, the woman's knees working loam into her skirt's brown and blue fabric, her green and maroon poncho gathering fragrance.

Today I take the dolls from the display hutch to smell Peruvian soil, its aroma still locked in tightly woven threads. I remember the child's quiet eyes resembling those of the dolls, dark and secretive, drifting like the Urubamba through the Sacred Valley past fortresses, terraces, rugged slopes this child has crossed in her bare feet.

I close my eyes, a blind woman, and forget the colors of the dolls, their faces shining in the dark as if the threads contain slivers of translucent glass. I touch tiny mounds: the eyes, bas-relief in cross-stitch, miniature moons tilted toward the figures' hearts, their heads and shoulders wrapped in heavy cloth, a protection from cold mountain air. The dolls' history comes to me through my fingertips: The town of Chinchero. A woman working rough-hewn figures from linen and straw, an Indian dreaming with her hands, as the child dreamed with hers, lifting her arms like a condor soaring through winds of the cordillera.

A Basket of Potatoes

*In the Andean heartland where potatoes
were first cultivated, they remain sacred
to the indigenous people.*

All evening I've been in the root cellar
laying out potatoes on a bed of leaves.

How ritualistic this seems, bringing in
the crop from earth where it cured

for three nights in the cold mountain air.
I want to dance barefoot on this altar,

squish liquid from the fleshy tubers,
squeeze the soft skins between my toes

like an Indian preparing *chuño*. In the late
hour, it takes so little to weave a spell.

The potatoes gather the room's dimness,
their eyes vigilant as the new moon slips

through the door's slats. I lean down
and steady a potato in a thimbleful

of radiance. The scrolls of its life
palpable, the eyes heavy-lidded, it opens

like a flower in my mind. I see again
a Quechuan woman shrouded and ringed

in a halo of the bountiful crop.
I remember offering my relative a prayer.

If only I could have given her a basket
of tranquillity: *papas de regalo*,

gift potatoes, yellow to deep purple.
Always, I dream like this until

the dead cross over to a place where
even a disbeliever begins to dance.

Song to the Sun God, Inti

Inti, lavish the earth: *espiritú del Lago
Titicaca, regalo de la Isla del Sol.*
Pierce the air with love arrows, air

woven through hair, soft alpaca wool
spun into gold by your seasoned hands.
Douse the *Yungas,* pour amber into fields

that women tend, their *borsalinos*
tilted like cups to catch light
sliding over curved rims into earth.

Soak papayas. Soak *maíz y las papas.*
Soak Machu Picchu, verdant in your arms,
its terraces alive from a windfall of yellow.

Bathe Scotch Broom on the banks of *Río Urubamba.*
Bathe cedar, mahogany, bamboo of the Amazon.
Bronze the bare skin of witch doctors.

Bronze their herbs and plants, help them
wipe out disease, fevers, viruses, the plague.
Heat the souls of macaws, parrots: blue-

green their wings, their flights aurulent.
Hold *mariposas* next to your prismatic heart.
Glisten in their flurry of colors.

Bathe *llamas, vicuñas, guanacos.* Shower
the doleful strains of *quenas, zampoñas.*
Tint reed boats ochre, the floating islands

of Titicaca. Dive through the lake's sacred
surface to the bottom. Warm the gold chain
of Huascar, flung there by the Incas

to protect it from the conquistadors.
Resurface and climb back into sky.
Regalo amarillo. Espiritú de todos.

Transparent Butterfly in Jardín de Mariposas

Wherever you land, earth turns green,
                                  wing-color, a gift
Quetzal sheds over you, sheen
                    of his feathers
                              falling as he lifts
through a hurrah of leaves.
                        Flutter, unfurl
                              your banners, wingspan red
as you flit above Bird of Paradise,
                        twirl
toward impatiens: blue, blue
                              seductive around your head.
What forest flower's spell
                          made you transparent?
Whatever you touch, you become:
                          leaf, stone,
passion flower. Nectar's scent
                    entices you, makes you visible
                    in sun's own
gleam. Butterfly,
                    find the shimmer of air
                            where fireflies hide.
Let them electrify
                you.
                          Your webwork dazzles
the forest you glide through.

In the Stonecutter's Workshop

Caught in a whirlwind, the animals feel
the stonecutter's hands twist and twirl

to shape their ears, legs, their dappled
faces. On the finishing table, an armadillo

spins, its armored back a charango, its ears
cocked to hear the strumming rise out of

its own body. The maker picks up a jagged
piece of tourmaline, carves a crocodile swishing

a monstrous tail, notched seven times to tally
the victims. Crystal becomes a condor,

wings glistening with light from the great bird's
heart. Quickly, the cutter moves his hands:

rabbit, duck, bear, squirrel growing out
of weary stones, broken-down, dim-colored

stones, victims of miners' picks and axes,
of the Stone God who in the beginning abandoned

these difficult stones. The creator turns an amethyst
over and over in his palm until a tree frog leaps

from a lavender forest. At daybreak when
his wife calls him to bed, his animals awake.

Wearing a cloak of gemdust, he ascends
the stairs with the air of Merlin.

FROM

Greatest Hits 1981 –2000
(2001)

Moonwatch

After Wallace Stevens' "Thirteen Ways of Looking at a Blackbird"

I.
The moon climbs out of the river.
A firefly stops his flight
beneath blood clouds
trailing for miles.

II.
Once, my belly hung
heavy with an imperfect motion
as though the moon, angry
and rotund, avenged my kind
for the generations behind us.

III.
Why are the Indian women
bowing before a temple light?
Do they know the moon
shrouds a mound, sacred
and well-hidden?

IV.
A man preparing to live
dies this way: climbing
into skies, swearing
the only light worth saving
is a delicate balance
he calls Moon.

V.
Children of Darkness, how long
have your eyes contained
the alterations of ancient moons?

VI.
The waters cover the shores tonight.
There is a Sea of Showers
in the moon's full light.

VII.
The moon crosses the ocean again.
Huntsmen lower their heads in prayer.

VIII.
When a woman's blood
darkens with imbalance,
she knows there will be no
moon that night.

IX.
The moon hangs cold
as the Mothers lay their offerings
upon a sacrificial ground.

X.
All night, tribesmen chant their hymns;
the old moon pales in the new moon's arms.

XI.
Sister, I am here beside the garden path.
I watch your spirit ascending
among the dusk clouds.

XII.
By the sanctuary door, I place twelve
silver jars in an arc of moon color.
Overhead, watchmen turn their lantern
toward the earth.

Donna Bruna

After Leonardo da Vinci's Mona Lisa, 1503-05
The enigma seems tied in with the landscape behind her.

What is your secret, donna bruna?
The countryside pulls greens of a lake
into the corners of your mouth.
The light hovers there, and it matters
that the road behind you spirals,
tapers off toward the west,
that a bridge softens curiously
against the deep curve of your back.

How calmly you accept this condition,
one hand crossing the other, light caught
forever in the folds of skin, caught
in the lunar precipices beyond.

*

The air clouds with mist,
and the landscape changes
to Florentine streets
where a woman smiles desperately,
radiant creature locked in a pose,
the artist painting
at the end of a road.

Femina scura, he should let you go.
The light vanishes from skies.
Your eyes fill with years.

*

Four centuries, and your eyes,
donna bruna, as intense
as the day the artist leaned
you against the studio wall,
your shadow cast upon the floor.

He should let you go.
Already, fog crosses the lake,
rising toward the veiled sky,
toward a woman running
over luminous hills
where the wind passes over
like a crazed bird, calling
no need, no need to turn back now.

The Replica

"No dolls live here. They do not walk
these palatial halls and chambers,
nor do they read. A shame . . ."
                    David Jeffery, "Royal House for Dolls"

For there are miniature books bound in leather,
a garden pergola, its trellis: a musical stave
carved deeply in an arched ceiling. And you,

moved by this pleasure, count
each rose, each blossom tilted
back, angled as a full note on the stave.

A comfort, the way you remember summer
flowers as a blessing, each petal tipped in a cream
or gold: I imagine a sonatina, the melody, long-held,

filling the royal house. There is a charm
about smallness, the way things take on dimensions
once reduced in size. Delighted, you stop

where orange tiger lilies, fuchsias, a ring
of toadstools grow in a garden so small
you take in the relationship of color

at a glance, while I remember years ago
the hunger in a man's eyes, how his blemishes,
inseparable from life, did not disappear

in death. How peaceful, looking now
into every room at once, no flaws,
the illusion from a craftsman's hand, clever,

each reproduction flawless on a smaller scale.
A shame: to isolate this house
from the dolls, who stare out

of glass cases in the outer vestibule,
whose eyes hold no light, lids
that will not close. I remember you looked

at the dolls, I waited, but the light would
not charm their features, the proportion
on a larger scale, less definitive, inexact.

Even then, I saw the man's face, the scars
he carried from birth, the emptiness
of another house.

I look at the arched ceiling: each rose,
a note filling the silence, and a light
that will not turn this darkness away.

Lately I Have Been Too Wrapped Up

in things, new job, new books,
new paints for the canvas, to let
the thoughts go until they settle

on something startling: this world,
for example, how it might be
otherwise if there were no colors,

if what came to us as the sea
were not blue, but a series of lines
you had to shape into swirling waves

to understand their essence.
I would cut fishline, tape it
to glass, then as a child might,

look through the surface
to the bottom. There would be Venice,
mosaic-goddess of the world,

found hundreds of years from now
at the bottom of the sea,
and in St. Mark's Square: a cathedral,

its walls and ceiling lined with stones,
faceted, ornamental stones in the shape
of Byzantine heroes. I would paint

the mosaics with water, let the Adriatic
Sea lap over their frosted surfaces.
On a day such as this, I do not need

to know colors to appreciate the property
of things. I can take a piece of string,
draw a basilica, look through its roof

to the inner walls where figures
touch one another and come to life
without the sun that lies

at the center of things
waiting to come to us
as coral, yellow, blue, or gold.

Apples

Today I'm thinking of apples,
a country kitchen, the smell

of pie cooling in the late
summer air. Let's say

it's evening, the hour
when anything's possible.

A small girl in a hammock
dreams of lightning: *poor will*

poor will, a horse's whinny
in the air. She wakes

to a wind, apples thrown
to the earth: succulent globes

that she rubs and rubs
until the world shines.

I'd like to say this happened
the first time a woman plucked

an apple and saw it as good.
I'd like to say she took the juices

of berries and painted a still
life that comes alive tonight

in the palms of a child,
the ripest fruit tilted

toward the light, ageless
and holding on.

Do You Know about the Rain Tree?

Do you know about the world's broad belt?
      They say that in Brazil at the equator
      birdsong fills the heart of the Catrimani
      River. Its bed, teeming with diamonds
      and gold, grows fat with this riot of light.

Do you know about the beehive tombs in Greece?
      Lower yourself by rope into the dark secret.
      If the rope breaks, let your eyes adjust
      to blindness. They say there is a sun
      behind your lids. Climb its ascending
      rays back to the earth's roar.

Do you know about the rainbow fish?
      Solid black, they ruled the waters
      before earthquakes opened their coffers,
      turquoise, topaz, amethyst, jade
      plummeting into the rivers where
      the eyes of the dark fish shimmered
      as they fed on the earth's rainbow.

Do you know about the hidden mountains?
      They say that in Tanzania and Kenya
      the mountains warred. Kilimanjaro
      and Mt. Kenya pushed their broad
      shoulders too high into sky.
      Now, whenever they nudge God's throne,
      his angry breath shrouds their peaks.

Do you know about waters of the Grotto?
      You will find the pool off the coast
      of Italy on Capri. Lie down
      in the boat's bottom to enter
      the cave's mouth, then feast on
      a blue mirror that butterflies
      carry here on their wings: pieces
      of sky they gather learning to fly.

Do you know about the rain tree?
        There's a tree, invisible, with a broad
        canopy in the sky. The earth sings to it
        whenever it's thirsty. They say
        if the song's loud enough to rise,
        the ripest blooms will break off
        their branches and rinse earth's
        green cathedral in firstlight and last.

Stones

You have just risen from night-
sleep. Opening a window,
you float above the city,

hear your lover cry out.
Startled by a brisk wind,
you remember a friend

stilled by cancer, how later
a stone filled your chest.
It's true, the mind says,

some stones carry magic:
Stone of Scone, Black
Stone of Mecca, even though

the hard mass extracted from
you held no spirits. It says,
the body made a terrible

mistake no hands can reshape.
You look at your hands, wonder how
they've taken marble, fashioned

a god so like the man who lowers
your gown and kisses the dark
scar, holds you all evening

while you rise above monuments
and touch his heart carved
deep in the crystal sky.

Among Cedars

a flute maker whittles.
Thick red slivers fall,
their scent so powerful
I'm again a young girl
opening the family's wooden
chest to savor a fragrance
that does not die out—
like the breath of the carver's
new flute becoming canyon
wind, rain burrowing
into corn's soil, flood water
paving rainbow's way.
The rough-hewn cedar
sings, and I take this
as witness of ancestral
presence, for I have come
to this grove to ask
my parents, long dead,
for a sign, that was here
all along in the stir of night.

On Sturgeon Creek

The osprey does not see me
follow its angular descent
for food: the creek's
surface breaks, gives way
to the claws' tug and pull;
the water stirs,
then stillness.

*Let nothing disturb
this peace,* I think,
leaning back in the boat
to study a crude nest:
twigs, branches, gathered
year after year, sun-
dried in a skeletal tree.

Now the osprey spots me.
Turning toward the sun,
the dark shadow fills
the eastern sky
and disappears.

*

No sign of the bird
who hours ago left shore
for the woods. I tell
myself, *Be patient.
Wait.*

*

Still nothing. No bird.
No strength to pedal home.
The creek's grown brackish,
and the tree tilts
the nest toward the boat.

*

The sun's going down,
and in the distance
the osprey heads
toward home. I close
my eyes, remember
standing in open
country, air thick
with the honey of day
lilies. Nineteen. I was
thinking of death, my mother's,
my own. I clasped the cross
I wore around my neck,
held onto it tightly.
I raised my head
in that field as I do
now to a different need.
Hush, the heart says.
The sky is lavender
and pink, and I have all
these years to praise.

FROM

River Country
(2008)

The Deserted Beach

I.
Not a hint of whistling wind
or a storm's kicked-up drizzle.
Or noisy beachgoers, their salty

backs turned toward clouds.
Where has everyone gone?
I search for a yacht or steamer,

for a tugboat, bobbing and yielding
to tides. What scared away
the creatures—a jarring undertow?

Did the sand crabs drown
in oily froth and gulls thrash
in heavens, curdled, unkind?

Something isn't right: eagles,
lost to these starved seas, clamor
elsewhere for waterfowl.

II.
The ocean unleashes its apathy
and softens to sapphire.
The horizon, electric as warmth,

rises from watery porticoes.
I pause to see what I missed:
the scuttle of shells, a belly

of sand between my toes.
The need to feel it: marvelous
swoosh of surf, breeze, and beach.

III.
Already they're returning.
The eagles soar, their cries
vanishing as secrets

in my cupped palms.
They hide beneath
feathery spume,

not even their shadows
visible. How easily
they tease me

into believing.
See crimson eve falling
in the shape of wings?

IV.
I marvel at the fullness
of a beach, deserted,
disguised as a path that pushes

eastward, the sandy shore
cobbled like plumage
of an elusive caracara.

Waves, milori-blue, cleanse
the heart and settle over all
things furtive. *Hear them?*

The eagles are headed south.
Tonight I will sleep soundly,
knowing they are safe.

Nest Building

"There are some enterprises in which a careful disorderliness is the true method."
                Herman Melville

The osprey soars through a cerulean sky,
scumbled with oyster pinks and whites.

Industrious, he scavenges insect carcasses,
sticks, seaweed, swells of twine, drops them

between the branches of a dead pine.
Melon light slides over his widespread wings,

over talons lowering twigs into the lopsided
nest. Shifting his weight, he shelters a jumble

of crosshatched twigs while house sparrows
flit in and out of leafy nooks. Back and forth

they zip, the hawk oblivious to the goings-on
in the basement, to the halo of bugs — ticks,

mites, larvae, drawn to fish-guts leftover
from a noonday meal. Back at shore, he shakes

off tawny flecks of matter before gathering
cornstalks to plump up his bulky home.

Four feet deep this week. Deeper next,
he boasts to himself, content to live

by the river's edge where trout are plentiful.
Puttering packrat, he'll forage again tomorrow.

His random collections tug at the soul,
call him back to this thriving creation,

aflutter with wiggles and squeals. Lit up
like spooned honey, he zeros in to land.

Dragon Run

Knee-deep in the Dragon, I lean in
        to feel the wilderness.

The brisk call of dawn splashes
        against ash and gum. Sassy,

this liquid sun pursuing a cypress,
        its roots lifted from the swamp

like stubby knees. Stooping, with the bowl
        of my hands, I draw from the depths

muddied snails, clams, a leech snaking
        palustrine waters and squirming as I fish.

Careful not to tear pickerel weeds
        or cattails, I let pliant grasses braid

the pristine path, nibble my manmade boots,
        gurgling through this sibilant stream,

swishing like a reptile. The windless
        air sliced, I search loblollies,

spy a bald eagle lifting off. Chiseled bones
        float by. Opiate: the thrall. I teeter,

fall. Against my jaw a damselfly's flutter.
        Like a stunned doe, I flail. The taste

of sediment numbs my senses. I breathe in
        these wetlands like a wild iris.

Elves

At first, I didn't see them, tricky thieves
of light, stealing forth on the backs of shadows

to deceive me. They were there in long shafts
of speckled red, mistaken for snapdragons, there

in the potpourri of roses and humming of bees.
How they carried on in the cove! Like acrobats

they swung through a willow's leafy canopy.
Hanging from slats of a makeshift bridge,

they disguised themselves in the swing and sway
of marsh grass. From a distance, I caught

a glimpse of their wild flight through sweet peas,
a leap into air enchanted by daylilies.

Along the wooded corridor, they slid over pathways,
slipped out of jackets, became jaunty viridian spots.

Near the gazebo, I knew they hid beneath
blanket flowers, geraniums, and nasturtiums.

Kneeling, I startled them to leaf tips:
glimmers all over this well-tended garden.

I welcomed their mischief into the studio.
They are there in the paintings, lively in play.

On the Studio-Boat

From the studio-boat I can see better: morning
haze, its ghostly vapor dissolving
into the river's mouth, plum-cloaked and opening

beneath the first light, ripples flooding
like sea pearls, pink and swelling.
I can see better from the studio-boat: morning

sweeping down, gulls gliding
over glassy surface, wing-shadows floating
into the river's mouth, wind-soaked and opening.

The suddenness of anything: a passing
jet, its ivory fumes parting.
I can see better from the studio-boat: morning's

masterwork, orchid winging
across sky. Maker of water diving
into the river's mouth, lavender and opening.

Skysails billowing, the day soaring.
A violin, the sun arrives, trilling.
From the studio-boat I can see better: morning
rises out of the river's mouth, wine-gold opening.

These Flecks of Summer

I.
Pink parasols everywhere:
mountain laurel releases
confetti at the feet
of two bickering cardinals
in a seed fight. Snaps one:
chip, chip. Cheer, cheer,
the other — their red robes
slapping the thicket.
Slicing into view, a third
bandit: black-barred, blue
as a Caribbean bay.
Another, another, the feeders
flutter: a woodpecker
feathers the angry boys.
The birds disperse.
Their fits and starts linger:
soulful like a rain-flurry.

II.
A storm pounds the peninsula,
summer's weather mutable:
one minute heavy showers
push through, the next:
a savory sun. Bees leave
the gazebo's eaves, swarm
toward begonias, their jubilant
dance giddy. Like gusts
of milkweed, they swirl.
Sticky nectar sugars
their tongues. Honeycombs
teem with amber sweetness
in harsh July heat
when the creek kicks up
steamy air and stirs the bees'
need to leave something
nourishing behind.

III.
All summer in woods
mountain laurel, hollies,
white oaks beg for rain.
Any amount will stop
their thirst, but ninety-
degree heat bears down.
June slips by, July creeps
to August, and then one day
drops fall steadily until
maples silver, the light
appearing in downpours —
replenishing amid the hum
of all things natural.

IV.
On loblolly-green, a frescoed
darkness falls, barely visible
in jacklight. Fireflies, lucent,
blink once, again. Split-second
later, mist showers wisteria,
catches moisture's unfurling
twirl, limbs braiding into ladders.
The yodeling moon climbs,
piggish for a slice of time,
for an hour or two alone
in storied skies without
freewheeling storms.
The moon pours over stubs
of zinnias, asters, sunflowers
that push through lampblack
soil, yielding to night's fragrance,
to her gloss and shine.

V.
Bearded irises appear,
jouvence-blue, and expand
their supple wings. Cut,
they spread throughout

the house in ornamental
porcelain. Regal
like guardians of dusk,
luminous lanterns,
they brighten the room.
Blue and pink-skirted
tulips and phlox,
shrill-voiced, trumpet
among leaves. On the table
by the stucco wall,
they step out, dazzling
in swift eddies of air.

VI.
Late August, my garden over-
flows: food for butterflies
and hummingbirds, blurry
slivers whittled and shaped
into stubby wings racing.
A hint of ginger, nutmeg,
sage, and I'm nourished
on profusion, wonder
which spices heal as well
as brisk showers, saucy
birdcall, honey-cinnamon tea.
By herb pots, I stoop,
fill jars marked *parsley,
rosemary, fennel*. For winter
I select the densest tufts —
soft as bearded irises,
as I imagine the expansive
moon is to the touch.
I'll sprinkle them over
salads, meats, fish:
these curative dried flecks
of summer, marsh-aqua
and bird-foot mint.

Solitude

River-darkness descends like a rite.
A resolute *kraa-kraa* unravels

the cloud-laden moon, picking
through thready reeds and cattails,

lambent in dusk. The marshes
murmur and swirl, startled

by the foot-stirring of a Great Egret.
Into rimmed air he glares,

alert for insects, crooks his neck
into a zigzag, and waits.

Loosening his breeding plumes,
he feathers shrub grasses,

his strong spear ready to plunge.
Bantam rays settle over plumage

of the bird stilled by a frog's croak,
by earth's heat dispersing night-croons.

In the shadows of laurel bushes,
I curl up like prey.

Skilled hunter, your golden
bill calls my name.

Hay Bales, Deltaville

*"A landscape . . . lives . . . by the air and light,
which constantly change."*
                Claude Monet

What is it about ever-changing light,
elusive as it falls on bundled grain,
altering the way we perceive the sight?

Bales, laced: the marbleized night
hovers above a dappled terrain.
What is it about the changing light

in moistened fields — the upright
stacks shimmering in feathery rain,
changing our perception, our sight?

Farmers, baling hay in late afternoon light,
witness how fleeting shadows sustain
a sunset's fire changing into night,

how a profusion of pink ignites
two misted stacks: the sheen, like porcelain,
changing again the ephemeral sight.

Evening's ponceau settles over bright
straw stalks, their burnt-orange hearts lain
bare by a burst of ever-changing light
shifting — Perceive it? — in clear sight?

Blood Moon

To see the full moon turn copper,
        drive to the end of a country road
                to a broad-mouthed bay

where darkness scatters stars
        like lit-tin
                across fields.

Wait until night dips
        like a tango, the steady hum
                of porch lamps forgotten

in the wailing of hounds.
        When the nip of chill
                mimics *tierra-lirra*,

pull umbral shadows
        closer until
                Cherokee Harvest

comes to you — Choctaw Blackberry,
        Hunter's, Blood Moon:
                brick-red.

Let celestial wines fill you
        with the power of tides
                swelling in channels,

inlets, coves, the rust-red
        of a fox, ardent as she laps
                a stream's lifeblood.

Be the terra-cotta disk fading
        to orange, orange
                to reclaimed white.

Dangle your feet over a dock's edge
        as the lingering trace
                of roan disappears,

Moon still visible in an unspoiled
        glow — and you in no hurry,
                no hurry at all.

Raking the Blues

Like a stirred fire, bronze
 tumbles over the back acre
where I'm raking and thinking

I'd rather be that sharp-shinned
 hawk overhead, squared-off,
red eyes riveted until

he swoops, feathers strewn
 at my feet, spotted, streaked.
Rather be that ground hog

munching corn, fattening up
 for the sweet sleep.
I'd rather be a wren, stubby-tailed,

make my home in a scooped-out
 nook. Rather be last June's
ruby-throated, tipsy from over-sipping.

Be a cowbird, laying eggs
 in a warbler's nest.
Make *her* raise my young.

Raking the blues, I'd rather not
 be squished pokeberries
or a granddaddy long-legs,

scuttling under leaves. Not be
 buckshot, a fleeting deer.
On the back acre I'd rather be

juniper, holly berry, a loblolly
 plume. Rather be a bunting
migrating. Be flying. Free.

On the back acre, raking, I'm whistling
 the blues. Rather be sprouting.
Leafing. Be greening. Spring.

By the Bay

How easy to become
a part of this fertile past:
a vast, amazed sky, gulls
billowing their small white
sails, caught in impetuous
breezes. To be here
beyond a peninsula's tip
and a temple of wind,
where an inlet's waters
wash over my feet,
the Chesapeake misting over
with the aura of coastlands.
I call out from this Point
as if expecting honey,
vanilla, and tobacco
from a passing ship
to blow ashore in boxes.
What is it about the Bay
that startles the heart?
The clouds' wealth opens
up, each drop cleansing:
all at once I am washed
in translucent wine.

Crossing a Rappahannock River Bridge

In memory of the bridge jumpers

I open myself like a clock
> *Maker*
and become a bridge jumper
> *of lost lives, I am*
hurtling over the edge: a wingless
> *gatherer*
gull swallowing the soaked air.
> *of scorned lovers.*
Blue roses fill my aching lungs.
> *Outstretched,*
My spindly legs fold, collapse
> *they fly:*
against a verdigris floor
> *hungry, lost birds:*
so alluring I imagine
> *warblers of woven songs.*
falling every time I cross this bridge.
> *Falcons,*
The glare on the surface calls.
> *tone deaf, wearied.*
I leap through cerulean
> *Gulls ablaze, fiery.*
haze that swirls, web-taut,
> *My tides swallow flames,*
around my waist, my heart
> *rocking.*
a jubilant ruby, my arms
> *Bruja, bruja,*
witch blossoms encircling
> *the spells, one by one, die out.*

this vast riverbed. Tuck away
                Earth angel, let go.
the desire, I tell myself,
                Fall into my currents, drifting
but the urge to fall, the urge
                just barely now.
to live like a cat back
                Live again
from the dead, the urge
                to feed on silken fish,
to feel the mighty stomach
                to feed on the bounty,
of water swells in me.
                to swim again.
Here, I am at home.
                Belong here
I am at home in the yawl
                in this curative grave,
of a meandering river,
                my dreamer,
in the comforting wetness,
                my watery child.

Elegant Worms

Thousands of C. elegans aboard the shuttle Columbia as part of a science experiment survived the crash on February 1, 2003. These pinhead-sized roundworms share many biological traits with humans.

The sky's an estuary blue
        Are we not like you?
when suddenly air sucks
        Many-celled,
thousands of you
        glowing,
through a bloom of particles.
        sensual,
You spiral downward
        sometimes slithery,
in a manmade coffin
        gliding,
that catches flashes of fire,
        we feed on
glints, metal bits
        rot and decay,
tumbling toward chaos.
        on earth.
All of you give birth
        We illuminate,
before dying, something
        brightening
to leave behind
        ourselves,
come spring when we open
        make
your silver-lined canister:
        more of us:
each of you under a microscope
        primitive,

smooth-skinned, cylindrical,
        rough-hewn,
tapered, elegant
        awake.
among rotting plants.
        Hear distant bells?
You thrive, granting us
        Honey-tongued,
wisdom in laboratories,
        roots of lilies
crusty black pearls
        call us
clinging to your shoulders
        to loosen
while you tug and pull
        red-bellied clay
at bruised vegetation.
        in the hollow dark.
How did you manage
        Blind,
the fall from grace?
        we saved ourselves,
Did you curl into yourselves,
        writhing
and in a freefall
        micron by micron
imagine a snake's charm
        from the wheeling fall,
and twirl? Did you clip
        recoiling,
pieces of shiny clouds to shape
        shutting down
into parachutes?
        into stasis,
Here in a Petri dish
        dormant

that fills and empties
>	*like death.*
with suppositions,
>	*We survived.*
you — tiny miracles —
>	*We — C. elegans —*
carry pieces of roots
>	*dreamed*
on your backs which bear
>	*lies,*
like strong rope your plunge.
>	*remained motionless*
Undeterred, you stir from sleep
>	*to stay alive.*
and go on with your lives.

The Jenny Dawn

The caretaker rubs grime from the Jenny
Dawn's salty planks like a farmer
scrubbing the flanks of his muddy horse.

> *Who woulda thought a nor'easter*
> *could ground her? One almost did*

Feeling an indrawn breath blow
off the Bay, he slips back in time,
finds himself aboard another workboat,

> *out near Tangier Island,*
> *where we was selling our catch.*

twang of her barrel chest cutting
the currents, while watermen, oystering,
pull yield, sort out empty shells.

> *'59's when the oysters took sick*
> *and died. Dredging turned real bad.*

Separating peelers and busters from soft-shells,
far-off the island boys crab. Nowadays,
pleasure seekers come to town,

> *Money being tight, some*
> *of the boys got caught poaching.*

longing for a sea romp aboard the Miss Lilly,
the Agnes, Lady Marion, and the Jenny Dawn—
city-bred folks who know nothing

> *About this ole deadrise – she'd a sunk*
> *all by herself if we'd done anything illegal.*

about the rustic tools it took to shape
these seafaring ladies so they could handle
the currents, draw up bushels of seafood.

> *There's few around here*
> *as loyal as the Jenny Dawn.*

'55 was one of the best yields.
The year before, Hazel had stirred up
creatures from the depths.

> *It'd take a roaring*
> *hurricane to ground her.*

Who would believe that a strong cleaning
could breathe life into this old girl?
Listen to her sigh like a wave's whoosh,

> *On the shallows, she fed*
> *the workers real good.*

like the cedars that gave her life
so she could gather the water's bounty.
All those trips into the rivers and Bay.

> *She'll never be like a beached whale.*
> *She's got the Chesapeake in her blood.*

Scrubbing, he listens to the rest
of her tales, the distant swells bluing
and the sky quiet like the eye of a storm.

The Revenant on Lover's Lane

In the 1800s a fisherman died of a fever
in the bedroom of his 19th century Deltaville,
Virginia home.
  L.B. Taylor, Jr., The Ghosts of Virginia

What thins the veil

    Feverish, I wander

between hours? Air,

     past you

bandaged like a shiver,

    like a ship's beacon:

pulls blinds up,

    troubled at sea,

slams the aluminum slats

   a revenant,

onto sills. Elusive,

    ill-starred.

it coughs, crouches low,

  Lying next to you,

turns door knobs

   unsettled,

until, pliant,

    can't you see me?

they click shut.

   I speak

Growling, it flicks

    your name.

the radio off. Air, quirky
>*Asleep,*

and brazen, scratches
>*you put*

on walls, slips down
>*my pleas*

odd-angled passageways,
>*aside.*

lined with photographs.
>*You dream.*

It trills the Victorian
>*Fenced-in,*

mansion with steely resolve,
>*my frame, weathered,*

thwacks headboards,
>*ruffles your bed shirt.*

wails like a squall, awakens
>*Frightened,*

the tenant, icy thrust of cold.
>*you shake off my being,*

Scuffling, it rushes by,
>*retreat*

elusive as footfalls.
>*to the fireplace.*

Blanched, it slinks
>*Gales rake the coast.*

from this residence
>*I am again*

on Lover's Lane,
      fishing,

lets loose its fever.
     chilled and sick,

No more wincing of air.
      longing for this room.

Hurricane

Where was fairness the night
your buckling gales snapped
the still-green trees?

Where was fairness
when woodland squirrels
wailed like brash screech

owls and deer lay paralyzed
in the heartless dark?
Was it fair to dream

of iridescent fields while
deafening whirlwinds
pillaged the land?

Fair to suffer a hurricane
twice: first as a frightened
child and again in autumn's rill?

Fair to rebuke you, tumbling
on your unwieldy path,
pushing turgid waters inland?

Fair to mull over your anger:
the jungle of pines, remnants
of homes washed to sea?

Fair to name you *consagrada
a Dios*? I remember squirrels
scampering in a flurry, their hurl

through branches of surviving oaks,
the unexpected dawn-struck glory
bowed to this thriving earth.

The Bay's Tributaries

It's not perfect living on a cove.
Sometimes it's sullied by runoff.

At low tide it empties to a mudflat.
High noon, the stench runs me indoors

to ponder matters: To spray or not
to spray the azaleas and roses, riddled

by burgeoning lace bugs and beetles.
To fertilize the lawn, weed-patched

after months of downpours. To consider
what the "Been Heres" say: *Ain't the way*

it sposed to be, builders puttin' up
too many of them waterfront homes.

I think about algae blooming close
to shore, about test-tube tumblers

of bedeviled water, and puzzle over what
to do: How to keep herons and ospreys

returning to these tributaries
year after year. Keep seasoned trees

alive with bird-bellow and blare.
Keep ooze and swale from swallowing

the Bay. Keep the drench and splash
wholesome, the wetlands yearning

for a willowy carpet. Keep
hummingbirds belling

their diminutive wings until
the toil of all that flapping

and sipping sugar-rich liquid
swells in the minds

of the "Come Heres" with a sweet,
translucent, pensive truth.

Caught Littering By the Law

Come on, son. Admit it. You've littered:
      styrofoam cup, tin can, maybe your little sister's
           disposable diaper that'll still be decomposing

in muck after baby's gone to dirt.
      I'll bet you've tossed fast food containers
           from the Get & Zip onto Stampers Bay Road.

That plastic jug yours, flipped out of this Chevy pick-up,
      racing this country road, 70 mph? You lazy
           good-for-nothing smoker, flicking that butt

like you're some King of the Road. I hear you:
      There ain't no toxic chemicals in them filters.
      Well, now, you're a *real* smart boy,

say around 17, 18? Cap on cockeyed, jeans frayed,
      tennis shoes mud-caked, soles worn down to nothing.
           Let me guess: headed for Gloucester to hang out?

Your mama know where you are, son? That you've taken
      to littering? How about we come out here tomorrow,
           and you clean up this stretch of road.

Look me square in the eye when I talk.
      Tail tucked between your legs real good now, eh?
           Well, maybe I'll let you off this time.

Maybe you've learned a thing or two.
      Land around here's for farming, boy.
           Dumpster's for trash.

Deforestation

"Look at the tsunami. Do you realize that almost every life that was saved was because somebody climbed a tree? But with deforestation, there were hardly any trees left."
      W. S. Merwin, *Poets & Writers*

What a gift to be saved by a tree.
In the South Seas, the roar
of waves deafened, but failed
to pull one tsunami survivor
from a sago palm's arms.
Five days later, fishermen
found her clinging to the ragged
girth, still gnawing on the tree's bark.

    *

Razed. Sacked. Across the waterfront,
the soil, fire-dinged, simmers.
Close to home, foxes, deer, raccoons
crave shade like a requiem.
You can hear trees — vintage
soldiers — slam to earth. No fanfare
about that. Nothing opaline
about a quick reduction to bare fields,
exposed: a slick, collapsing green.

    *

Where I used to live in Burke,
the trees cowered in tainted air,
skeletons of former selves
that once muscled their way
into D.C., into Dumbarton Oaks'
solitude, into Rock Creek Park's
ravines and hills, into summer's
leafing of the city's breathing chapel.

    *

Now, near an isolated cove
off the Piankatank River,
I put out cracked corn
for the doves among stands
of tulip poplars, ablaze
by the feeders. Errant acorns
sprout, the lawn a stubbled beard
of plenty. Out of loblolly thickets,
a fox kit appears, skittish but attuned
to her territory where nature thrives
unchecked. If only I could steady
this scene: the kit in a windbreak
of pines, wild berries dribbling
down her chin, and the country
air we take for granted, teasing
our hearts beneath a missive sun.

*

Evensong. The natural world
praises itself: great horned owl's
low *hoo, hoo-hoo* and heron's hoarse
squawk, birds visible to the ear,
leafy canopies their screens.
Cut the trees for a better view,
we're advised but prefer it this way—
laurel's leaf-razz: a fox.
Slivered roars: herons lift off.
Peals of *coo, coo, coo*:
doves on a high branch.

*

Most afternoons on the edge
of our woods, a raccoon burrows
for bounty, stashed by a fox.
Animals come and go as they please.
They scramble to survive.
Plenty of massive trunks to hide
behind when we appear.
Every day I become more nearsighted
as the clamor draws closer. I look
around me. Trees hard at work
sculpt the air we breathe.

Green Burial

"By setting aside woods for natural burials, we preserve it from development . . . and put death in its rightful place, as part of the cycle of life."
        Dr. Billy Campbell, founder of Memorial
        Ecosystems, Westminster, South Carolina

Do not embalm me.
Leave me unclothed.
Vegetal soil will be
my dress, the resolute
night my swanky coat.

A simple coffin please:
pine, softened
and carved
by hearty rains.

Bury me in a natural
setting beneath
a hickory, maple,
or oak. No headstone
looming like a garret
or my name hollowed
in petrified stone.

No fumbling eulogy
to blemish the sanguine
air. No effusive tears
on my behalf.

Drape the woods
with a flute's voice.
A mockingbird's reply
will tunnel through
a tangle of vines.

Lay a colony of clover.
Plant saplings near
the mound. The ground
will teem with sweet-
showered cypress,
holly, and willow green.

In time out of loosened
loam, I'll sprout
my fledgling limbs.
Grant me these tidal
sails. Let them billow
in emerald winds.

FROM

The Embrace: Diego Rivera and Frida Kahlo
(2013)

DIEGO RIVERA
1886 – 1957

"I . . . discovered an enormous artistic reservoir. It was of the kind that enabled the American genius Walt Whitman to create, on a grander scale than anyone had before, the poetry of the common people, working, suffering, fighting, seeking joy, living and dying." [1]

Diego Rivera,
My Art, My Life: An Autobiography
(with Gladys March)

Diego and Calla Lilies

       Kneeling on a petate mat,
The basket, deep enough,
       an Indian woman sits upright,
supports our long, firm stems.
       her unclothed frame scented.
We settle into clots of dirt.
       Is it sandalwood? Mahogany?
Like absinthe, we intoxicate
       I paint her broad shoulders:
the artist who shapes the woman's arms
       earthy dabs of nutmeg, hyacinth
with the mastery of sun
       so she can thrive like the flowers,
so she can embrace us.
       so she can feel the florets swell.
Her hands, smelling of freesia,
       Soon, she will rise out of shadows
reach out to our trumpets blaring
       to gather bluets, yarrows.
as though she hears a mariachi horn,
       What is happiness, if not this need?
feels our desire to return to marshes,
       See how she rests – a saint – holding
watery fields, shallow pools far from
       pearls, luminous as fire?
the lover who approaches a street vendor—
       Now, maybe you understand who I am.
scissor snips ringing through the market,
       In the city, in the valleys,
fleshy tubes and arrow-shaped leaves
       I wander in search of legends
rolled into wrapping paper, sold for a few pesos,
       to begin anew. Oh, these calla lilies!
the blooms' swanlike hearts pounding.

Halley's Comet

In the Gallery of the San Carlos, Diego Rivera's first one-man exhibition opened on November 20, 1910 – the same day the Mexican Revolution broke out with an uprising against the dictator, Porfirio Díaz.

I.

You gloat at the Opening. Regal, prim,
the dictator's wife buys six paintings
and toasts your success. *The Valley
of Ambles* and *The Tranquil Hours*
belie the tension mounting outside
the city among *campesinos*. To think
that years later you would lie, claiming
you intended to assassinate Díaz,
claiming Lenin needed you abroad
to arbitrate among Mexican factions.
Could you not own up to the truth?
In May, I soared through skies over
Mexico, warned your countrymen
to heed the unrest. Some called my
fiery appearance an omen. You,
Diego, were in Paris. With an eye
averted, you painted long into night.

II.

Look at you, *muy importante*
in a tailored suit. Your bulging
eyes pierce holes into a critic
who barely notices your art.
Go ahead. Cast him off
as you later would Angelina,
who bore your son, and Marevna,
mother of the baby you labeled
child of the armistice. Do not
ignore me. Others before you
have been this careless. In 66 AD,
I steered ships off course.

1066, I flew over England,
cursed Harold of Hastings.
In the 1300s, I posed as Giotto's
Star of Bethlehem, curved
like a saber over the Nativity.
Each time I reappear, I make
a more powerful showing.

III.

Egotistical. Quarrelsome.
The devil is in the room, Diego.
Mask after mask you wear
like armor. As a boy you opened
the stomach of a pregnant mouse,
played with your brother's corpse —
you claimed — at a wake.
What do you say now to a child
soldier who bears arms, stumbles
over bodies in barren fields?
How many etchings, drawings,
oils did you bring here to please
la crema de la sociedad?
In a corner of the gallery, patrons
surround one of your masterpieces,
admire the rotund face staring back.
You lift a glass to the hostess, guests,
to the long life of Don Porfirio.
How can you ignore the cries
of the dead rattling the windows
of this sumptuous hall?

From: **Murals**

In 1923 Rivera began painting 124 frescoes on three floors of the Ministry of Education building in Mexico City. These murals reflect the Mexican people at work, their land, struggles, triumphs, and festivals. Rivera longed for a day when everyone would exist in harmony, without class distinctions.

I.   Entering the Mine

A rooster's crow swallows what's left of night.
        The lantern I clutch flickers as I enter
                the hill's gashed belly.

I offer a blessing to the underworld, pray
        to its ruler. *No need to take chances*,
                I tell myself, swinging a pick

into rich veins of silver. The stench
        of Devil's breath fills my lungs.
                I cough. I remember Papá

hovering over my bed and kissing
        my forehead. "Don't follow me
                into the mines," he warned.

"The fumes will turn your lungs to stone."
        A five-year-old, I squeezed
                his hand like a treasure.

At fourteen, I toiled in fields, built up
        my muscles until they commanded
                crops like rain filaments.

At eighteen, I followed Papá through narrow
        streets to the mines, bowed my head
                before descending,

each of my brothers heaving a wooden beam
        as if carrying the cross of Jesús.
                Now, I lean against a rugged wall,

take shallow breaths, tell myself the stale air
        won't harm me. I stare into darkness,
                see again my father slumped

in a corner like a pile of dirt. This time
        he doesn't speak but floats
                toward me, a banner unfurling.

From its seams, water pours over crude,
        rough nuggets. I touch his blackened
                fingers, shout his name

into the moonless night as we lift him rung
        by rung up the ladder. His lantern flares
                like fire. *Mi padre. Mi padre.*

II.   Leaving the Mine

Again you search me.
        With your cartridge belt
                clanging against your hip,

you are no better. You probe
        each miner until someone
                hands over the stolen silver,

which you'll steal yourself
        when no one's looking.
                I am nothing to you,

a poor worker longing
        for a few pesos. Bread
                the color of your shirt.

Beans lampblack. Corn
        sweetened by the sun-drenched
                rays I long for

in the tunnels of this open pit.
        I raise my arms into granite
                sky, my frame posed

like a crucifix, my sandaled feet bleeding.
        Beneath your leather boots,
                my brother clings to a rope-

and-timber ladder, his face ashen.
        Hunched over, you frisk my flanks.
                The stench of tobacco

carries me back. My father had arrived
        home late. "A boulder the size
                of this room," he said,

"collapsed into fistfuls of ore."
        As someone dragged Papá
                through a narrow hole, he closed

his eyes and dreamed of gold and silver
        ready to mold into coins, each adorned
                with the coat of arms:

an eagle gripping a snake in its beak.
        Hoisted to the surface and stripped,
                he barely felt the hands

of the light-skinned man run up and down
        his naked thighs. Papá should
                have shaped the metals

into shining swords, sharpened them
        until they slid like a curse
                through the guard's ribs.

III.   Hymn: The Embrace

Embrace the land, my brothers.
    It will sing to you of stony hills
        sheltering the tremulous night,

of rivers, belling slopes, a flute's
    voice in moon's wail.
        Sing of you, *mis hermanos,*

come together in the saintly dark.
    Embrace the land gone fallow, scorched
        fields, dust-laden rows.

They will sing to you of ill-starred
    crops, the curdle of worms,
        brambles, an owl's screech.

Sing of a farmer's howl
    in the dead of day.
        Embrace the land, gentle

peasant and urban worker.
    It will sing of consoling rains,
        the descent of amber rays.

Sing of a halo in the shape
    of a sombrero wreathing
        your heads, bowed as one.

IV. Offerings, Day of the Dead

There's nothing morbid about death,
        yet here your family sits: spectral,
                downcast as if the spirits

are late, figures adorned, ornamental
        paper cut like Posada's skeletons,
                like lace and strung

in bourgeois finery while tapers
        burn, fill the cemetery
                with the absence of praise,

lost promises on an altar. Weightless,
        they enter through cracks
                of earth, become their former

selves while you, content to share
        this bounty, pray and offer
                pescado y pollo picante

to deceased relatives who'd rather
        once a year eat sugar skulls
                with icing, with the scent

of incense adorning the bones.
        Stop frowning. Caress them.
                La calavera catrina taps

on headstones as the sportive angels
        take down the imposing wreaths,
                snuff out candles, admire

their portraits tidied with a wealth
        of marigolds for as long as
                danza de la muerte lasts.

V.   Bread

"Now they have bread for all,
the naked, the men at the bottom . . ." [2]
      From: *"Corrido de la Revolución"*

Partake of the wheat.
        Break into morsels and eat.
            Break grain, whole meal,

graham, rye. Tongues of flour
        baked to a nut-brown.
            Bread splits in two

at the fire's pleasure. Bread of the fields,
        scattered to crows and tossed
            to the aqua birds.

With the first taste will come
        pineapples, papayas, peaches
            the size of your hand, milk

flowing from a split coconut's cup.
        With the taste will come a platterful
            of cheeses, jugs of honey

the shade of umber flesh. Give praise.
        Partake of wheat's breath.
            Bread of your lips, shaped by gods.

Eat to the full: tortillas, *pan rustico.*
        Leavened, kneaded: bread of dawn.
            Pillars of yeast, rising, rising.

Wives

"I, unfortunately, was not a faithful husband.
I was always encountering women too desirable
to resist." [3]
>Diego Rivera, *My Art, My Life: An Autobiography*
>(with Gladys March)

I.   Angelina Beloff

In France, I fell in love
          with the robust artist.

Though he rarely spoke of marriage,
          one day he surprised me

with a wedding ring—
          a gift from his mother.

I asked how he could cherish
          a woman he refused to wed.

Annoyed, he turned his back
          and resumed sketching.

In time, my belly grew.
          After the child's birth,

if the baby whimpered, Diego
          threatened to get rid

of him. In the studio,
          self-absorbed, he cursed

anyone who interrupted him.
          First bronchitis, then flu

sickened our Dieguito.
          You would have thought

a father, out of decency, would
          remain by his son's bed.

Instead, he reveled for days
          with friends in bars,

lifting a beer to Cubism.
          When our boy died,

who do you suppose
          suffered most?

I do not want to sound offensive.
          Diego is not vile.

He simply cares more for his art
          than for any woman.

II.   Lupe Marín

As a husband he was attentive—
    in fact, very manly.

But he ignored paying bills
    and seldom bought food.

He preferred to dole out money
    to the Communists

and splurged on hand-carved idols.
    He never lavished our girls

with gifts. We parted because
    he cheated on me

with a model. I was angered
    by this lack of respect.

Because he was well-known,
    rich women adored him.

And yet he rarely took a bath.
    He washes daily now

because he's older, and to gain
    a mistress he must cleanse.

Over the years I've forgiven
    him for his dalliances.

The only woman who matters
    to Diego is his muse.

III. Frida Kahlo

In twilight's crimson, Diego
pillows against my breast,

wraps the legend of amaranth
around my shoulders. I become

his mother. He, my child,
a *sapo-rana*: a toad-frog

with sagging skin. "Fisita,"
he sings, his large-set eyes

droopy, "you are a sparrow
soaring, your eyebrows feathery,

close-knit." He is my universe,
the meandering stars. I, his spider

monkey, lunge from tree to tree.
But my Buddha is never all mine.

A mask, a headdress: my refuge.
I embrace dogs, an eagle,

parakeets, macaws. I endure
his cathedral of blood-red lies.

His little Demerol girl
in a dead sleep flirts with lions,

black angels with broken
wings. I, the breath of rose,

the fragrance of lust. He is
my destiny, the whistle of wind.

IV.   Emma Hurtado

The sky opened like a Spanish fan.
        Party hats covered the horns

of bulls tugging fiesta wagons.
        El Popo in the distance

spewed a shroud over the plain.
        Throughout the ceremony,

clouds split into crinkled confetti.
        We embraced, and it was over—

no witnesses, our wedding kept
        secret for a month.

        *

A lump hardened, burned, sickened
        Diego, his forehead

creased from worrying
        about a cancer so bold

he couldn't stare it down.
        "Will you go with me

to a country," Diego asked,
        "where blooms of cobalt

can cure?"   A blur, the long days
        in a Russian hospital.

Nights coalesced into fists
        that pounded at the wound.

Women doctors showered him
        with attention.   I didn't mind.

For a man with a heart like his,
        he needed his emotions fed

so he could paint twilight over seas
        pure as dahlias, opening.

        *

In April, they told us he was cured,
        but his failing eyes closed

as if he saw the mysteries within,
        as if he heard a lark's

doleful notes. Alone, he traveled
        to Guanajuato, weeping

as the town's ghosts spilled
        out of crumbling mines,

out of hills that lifted spirits into
        indigo skies of his youth.

        *

I dreamt his soul floated
        over the boyhood town.

The sound of blood leaving
        his veins filled the streets

as his small hands painted sunsets
        too durable to fade.

I smoothed the sleek hair, wiped
        furrows from his brow.

        *

I was never envious of his success
        or of the other women.

His inability to make love
 these past few years

never mattered. His eminence
 as an artist shields him.

FRIDA KAHLO
1907 – 1954

"I am not sick. I am broken. But I am happy to be alive as long as I can paint." [4]

Frida Kahlo: The Brush of Anguish
by Martha Zamora
(Trans. Marilyn Sode)

Frida and Wet Nurse

You do not nourish me, though you offer your breasts,
   A wet nurse,

while my real mother gives birth to a sister.
   I do my duty. I sacrifice

Your milk bitter as oleander, I call you Nana.
   a suckling infant at home,

I'd rather press my lips to clouds drizzling
   shedding tears

over a maze of leaves, engorged veins
   buoyant as breath.

feeding insects, giddy with song.   Newly born:
   Wiggling, you turn from me,

a praying mantis, a monarch sucking fluid from stalks.
   obsidian eyes, empty.

Estranged, I refuse to knead your chest,
   Disheveled universe,

releasing drops into my half-opened mouth.
   crack open this shield.

Indian woman, why won't you remove your mask?
   Reorder this life

As moon candles the stars, cradle me
   saturated with providence

so I can fold back time and dream my mother
   among splashes of rain,

nurses me, her milk—consecrated by a kiss—
   spilling from a holy font.

The Wedding Fiesta

I.

In a native skirt, blouse and *rebozo*
borrowed from the maid, I married
Diego in a civil ceremony.
Thinking it insane to choose a man
old enough to be my father,
Mother refused to attend the wedding.
Nothing will destroy my mood,
I thought, until I arrived at the fiesta.
Ex-wife Lupe hoisted my skirt,
ridiculed my limb crippled by polio.
I knocked her off-balance.
Diego pulled us apart.
Dispirited, I drank like a mariachi
and sang above the band
while Lupe's tiger howl dissolved.

II.

Nothing will destroy my mood,
I vowed, as I consumed oyster stew.
Stimulated by mollusks, I eyed
the multi-layered cake, a sugar-paste
couple on top, white-icing doves
lording over saffron rice, stuffed
chilies, spicy *mole* sprinkled
with sesame seeds. The alcohol
and roar of trumpets dulled
my senses. Above the balcony
amid lingerie hung out to dry,
an ornamental pennant flapped:
"Long Live Love!"

III.

My marriage has always been
wound tight like my art: *a ribbon
around a bomb,* Breton said,
magic and heartache blended.
As the party ended, I appeased
Diego by feeding him watermelon,
thin slivers of papaya, the black
seeds: temptresses luring him
like wide-eyed brides-to-be.
I thought nothing could destroy
my spirit, but as days turned
to weeks, I woke frightened
at seeing life split open. Scorned,
I separated into *las dos Fridas.*
A heavy pall of smoke descended
as the clock ticked down.

The Two Fridas (I): On the Border Line Between Mexico and the United States

I stand on a pedestal before the Ford factory,
    Waving a Mexican flag,
clinging to the possibility of a better life,
    I pause on the border line,
my bold cigarette, fingerless gloves,
    head slightly turned,
coral necklace something to gossip about
    my culture ignored
at fancy parties, thrown by industrialists.
    in Gringolandia,
By day, bosses blare commands at workers.
    the atmosphere smug.
I do not belong in Detroit with its smokestacks
    Far from the temple of gods,
and skyscrapers, iron-gray, devoid of windows.
    far from my collection of idols,
Diego perches for hours atop scaffolding,
    I pine for volcanic stone,
adorning walls with the churn and grind of machinery.
    for the budding cactus and jasmine
How can he claim the human spirit thrives here,
    spinning roots through soil.
his message throttled by censorship?
    After the miscarriage I disappeared
On the edge of his life, I replicate
    in sun's fiery throat,
a brick building against a landscape cluttered
    the quarter moon lost in a blur.
by chimney stacks, their robotic appendages
    Hanging onto my past,
stretched-out, this country's flag
    I ignore the stars and stripes.
rippling overhead in dense smog.
    I cling to green, white, red.
I operate like a generator. Plugged in, I march
    In a frilly, pink dress, I rouge my cheeks
on command to orders barked on cue.
    and light up this dirty little stage.

The Two Fridas (II): Collage, Manhattan

I can't bear another minute of these
>*Pretentious snobs,*
gringachos putting on airs over cocktails.
>*the big shots crave liquor.*
I hunger for Mexico's exotic cuisine,
>*I thirst for lime water,*
for quesadillas, spun from squash blossoms.
>*a dessert of mango sorbet.*
In Manhattan an arctic chill descends,
>*In a collage, I paste*
Wall Street's Federal Hall looming dead-center.
>*a church, a stained-glass window,*
While Diego kowtows to American progress,
>*serpentine $ around a cross,*
I pay homage to socialites for their perfect
>*fuel pumps, smokestacks,*
plumbing: lid propped wide-open on a toilet.
>*a thunderhead grabbing the fumes,*
Hats off to the sports hero, posing as a trophy,
>*a movie star, glamorous,*
gold-lit on a column. Hats off to the telephone,
>*aloft a faded dwelling,*
wires winding through buildings like nooses.
>*the windows grim.*
For the millions earned weekly,
>*On the inaugural site, I paste*
hats off to the moneybags. Lined up, the masses
>*George Washington, stoic,*
protest the city's waste, its spent greed spilling
>*patriotic reds weaving*
from a garbage can. Hats off to the system
>*throughout the city.*
that gobbles up the poor like candy.
>*I don't care to be somebody.*

Against skyscrapers I hang my ruffled costume,
                I could care less about socialites.
dangling like an albatross. How like Lady Liberty
                Shrouded in fog,
to wave absently. How like her to keep her distance
                the harbor statue disappears,
from the lonely and forlorn.
                her eyes shut to a passing ship.

The Two Fridas (III): Sitting on a Wicker Bed with Ceramic Doll

Nothing but drab walls, barren.
    An idle toy bed
No paintings or pottery. No clay gods
    shoved in a corner:
lining the terra cotta floor. No children
    no figurines
feed my needs. And so I collect dolls,
    fill the empty cradle
redo ragged bodies, top each one
    with a celestial smile
with a miniature wig, silken hair
    plucked from air.
from a cherub. Destitute, I sit upright
    No baptismal gown,
on a wicker bed, hued by humidity.
    no tiny shoes to coddle.
Stale cigarette smoke clings to my skin.
    Tucked away, a fetus in a jar:
You ask how I'm doing, my only companion
    an ungodly curse
in this room: ceramic, unclad,
    holding me captive
its oval eyes begging me to lower my blouse
    and not letting go.
so its lips can draw nectar from my nipples.
    I invoke a saint
Cruel Diego turns a blind eye. I refuse
    out of unenviable grief.
to hold the inanimate object. Can't the Maestro see
    I wait for the lilt of day.
I need more than dogs, a deer, my countless dolls?

Frida Dialogues with Her Heart

Is it Diego who slices me
       I want to cut him,
from the body, or did you
         hollow each chamber,
crop your raven hair short,
       cast him aside like spoiled meat.
manlike, and then slash me
        I want to rip out my heart,
from the chest? Iron-red streams
       feel nothing, all those women
pour into the ocean
         in his lustful embrace.
and flush to sea. I am
      No longer clothed like a Mexican,
still beating: a nautilus
        I abandon him,
cast ashore. My melodies
     flee to New York City,
fade as you break down—
        take lovers: men, women.
your school uniform and
      I want to hurt him,
native garb dangling from ropes.
        but what does he know of pain?
Wearing a plain skirt,
      My foot bandaged, toes gone,
a tawny jacket flashy
        at times I dress like a man,
with splotches of white, you
    roam streets,
do nothing as clouds pull
        my dreams without him:
demons into shivering sky.
    center stage.

Let me back inside. Let me
        Long into night
sever the cords
      I drink brandy,
holding your beloved apparel,
        curse my sister for giving in
throw out the liquor, lovers
      to his advances.
doleful cries. Do not
       Heart. Oh, Heart.
abandon me like an Aztecan child
      Tear yourself free
sacrificed to the gods.
        so I can live again.

The Two Fridas (IV)

As a child I met my imaginary friend
    I have always known there are two of me:
in the earth's core. O how she made me laugh.
    Dark-skinned Mexican. My German self,
Before each secret romp, I blew on a window
    strong-willed, blouse ripped open, heart undone,
in my room, the pane misty like blurry soap bubbles.
    scarlet flowers smeared on my skirt,
With my fingertip I drew a door, jumped through
    its alabaster landscape stained. I clamp a vein.
to Pinzón. Entering the store's giant O, I crawled
    My indigenous sister clasps my hand,
into world's interior where a playmate opened her arms,
    her other hand encircling a portrait: frog prince,
listened to my secret problems, consoled me,
    Diego as a boy. He lusts for the Mexican.
made me laugh despite my burdens.
    His soul's yoked to hers. That's
When it was time to leave, I erased the magical door
    what tears us apart: veins, tethered, choke me,
from the glassy surface. I wandered to the patio
    our lives: aborted and miscarried.
to sit beneath a cedar tree's dancing shadows
    Stop this flow of shared blood. Loosen this grip.
to conjure her up again, sturdy as breath.

The Two Fridas (V): The Wounded Table

*". . . behold the hand of him that betrayeth me
is with me on the table."* Luke 22:21

I was 33 when Diego requested a divorce.
                    Notice innocent

Time stopped at 2:53. Today I sit
                    children and a fawn nearby,

at the center of a wooden table, surrounded by
                    a terra cotta idol, peg legged –

remnants of a faltering life:
                    a papier-mâché Judas,

my sister Cristi's adoring children.
                    the sky heavy with clouds

My pet deer Granizo, his spots tiny
                    like puddles of hailstones.

like bread scraps. It is dinnertime, but I refuse to eat.
                    Notice how Judas's arm caresses me

Nor do I speak to the giant figure to my right,
                    as if flirting with death,

clothed in overalls, hands flattened on the surface.
                    droplets oozing from the laced ruffle

I am one with the Pre-Columbian idol to the left.
                    of my mestizo attire,

A skeleton entwines my unbound tresses around his wrist.
                    my wounded right foot hidden,

I refuse to give in to the harsh yank
                    the tabletop's piney knots wine-stained

or to care about blood pooling around the feet
                    as if bludgeoned,

of my companions. This is how my husband leaves me:
                    a stigma. Marked like a leper,

abused by a predatory disease. I reach out
   I paint the frailty of my condition.

of my stupor, tug at the ponderous curtains until
   I am surrounded by Diego's artifacts,

the tassels loosen and the burgundy sheaths fall,
   a sacrificial fawn,

innocent as lambs, the passion play
   no bread, no wine.

welling up inside me like a betrayal.
   How could he undo me?

The Two Fridas (VI): Broken Column and Plaster Cast

Fragmentos, that's all that remains of my spine,
crumbling like an ancient column.

>   *I swab a plaster cast with yellow,*
>   *violet, and mercurochrome.*

Confined by a rigid brace, I look into a mirror,
iron nails boring their precision into flesh,

>   *I dab red paint on the surface until*
>   *a hammer and sickle shine.*

the pupils of my eyes strained, tears blurring
my sight. Two doves stare back.

>   *Caged, I embellish each prison*
>   *made of leather, metal, or plaster.*

How tired I am of surgeons tearing me
apart with their opinions and solutions,

>   *To place me in a corset, doctors*
>   *suspend me from a cable.*

splitting open the torso to reveal burdens I bear.
My husband's seldom at home, his art a ruse

>   *I lose consciousness and imagine Diego*
>   *sketching a model draping herself,*

luring him to paint long hours while I stand
here, nearly naked on the vast desert plain

>   *swirling a sheet around the body*
>   *this simple, yet modest movement*

he adores, white cloth draped over
my longing, earth's floor fractured

> *a siren's call to a life made of steel.*
> *I listen to my world shattering.*

as if by an earthquake. How demanding
to play the role of a brave child.

> *I call out to the void, wait*
> *for the solace of an echo.*

Why can't I collapse
like the fabled ruins of antiquity?

The Two Fridas (VII): Paint Me Flying

"It is certain they are going to amputate my right leg . . . .
I am very, very worried, but at the same time
I feel it would be a relief." [5]
    THE DIARY OF FRIDA KAHLO, August 1953

Paint me flying through saffron skies:
                      Feet — why do I want them?

a hummingbird, wavering like a supple leaf.
                      Wings are enough.

Balanced on a sliver of dawn,
                      I'll wear a wooden leg

I'll hover among trumpet vines.
                      and twirl on a dare —

Paint me curled up in a seamless knot:
                      among honeysuckle, bee balm —

a hairless caterpillar on a pansy's back,
                      slender as a flicker.

waving its gilded wand until a butterfly flits.
                      I'll don leather boots,

Paint me reclining on a mandrake's tongue,
                      cerise aflame,

stout as a root. Paint me ascending, a parrot
                      graced with bells.

from a basket of berries, luscious in a heap.
                      If I have wings,

Píntame volando, a dragonfly plaiting the air.
                      what do I need feet for?

Letter to Diego

What is it that connects us? You said
you loved me in my Tehuana dress.
You said you loved my black hair
secured with steel-red ribbons and combs
and buckling like a braided snake.
How long did it take you to become
a maelstrom around my neck, swirling
waters spun into a silken noose
and tightening? I cannot deny my anger.
Your world teems with other women:
your model Nahui, then Cristina, my own
sister. How could you? The thought
of you sleeping with others changes
my heart into an hourglass that empties
into the veins of every woman
you've bedded. I cannot deny my hurt.
You gave me child after child, each torn
from my womb, umbilical cords spiraling
out of me like groundless roots.
After my third baby died, the doctor
cut off my toes while you, selfish
and callous, painted pretty Cristina
into your *Epic of the Mexican People,*
her two children seated beside her
covering me with their oblivion.
And so I loosened my long hair,
sheared it to take you down with me
where I lay exposed, blood-splattered.
How much can a person endure?
I lie, immobile, in my four-poster bed,
the past unraveling like one of your murals.
Some people suffer a single tragedy,
but I have suffered two. After the first—
a bus accident—I remember hearing
voices, a handrail piercing my body,

the severed organs spilling
a communion of blood. You, Diego,
are my other tragedy. I would tear you,
piece by piece, from my heart,
but I have nearly lost my soul.
I can no longer bear loneliness,
your affairs, your lies. And yet—
my leg shorn from me like a lost ribbon,
my spine a withered branch—when I die,
I will fly back to you on gilt wings.

The Crematorium at the Panteón Civil de Dolores

I.

Never question my power
or assume I delight in what I do.
I can excite, ignite, or illuminate
bodies. For hours, they burn
with a fervor that reduces
to an impenetrable gray mass.
Do not label the remains "ashes."
Gather a fistful of these bone
fragments, ground into a fine
substance sacred as dust.
Place a loved one in a treasured
cloth to preserve in a cedar box
where memory cannot die
until mind or time releases
it from your grasp.

II.

Resting on a cart, Frida Kahlo
approached the oven with royal
dignity, her headband lined
with carnations scarlet as roses,
a shawl gracing the sloped shoulders.
When they rolled her through
my doors, a blaze roared,
thrust her upright, hair haloed,
the vermilion scars all over
her back aglow. Like a phoenix
she burned. The ardor of her
trembling built to a crescendo
as the inferno intensified,
her face a sunflower in bloom.
Once the flames subsided,
her skeleton emerged,
intact, lustrous as silver.

III.

Unlike the arsonist who derives
pleasure from torching, I value
the artistry of fire and consume
those disfigured by disease
or injuries too severe to mask.
I ignite the forlorn and those
who cannot bear lying
prone for eternity.

IV.

Who can fault Diego for
sketching the filigreed bones?
No longer confined to a bed,
Frida burned with zeal—
no need for vibrant jewels,
skirts trimmed with flounces,
no want of *huipiles* or hair
plaited with ribbons and flowers.
In the comfort of an oven,
she became whole again.

La Casa Azul

Blue, the aura of my walls: a deep-matte
    añil so intense it wards off evil.

Nothing can compare to this uncloaked
    hue, neither Michoacán earthenware,

nor sapphire streamers billowing
    from beaks of papier-mâché jays.

Neither floating teal boats nor hand-blown
    royal goblets can compare

to the spell I cast: *añil* regal in *retablos*
    and gossamer in glazed Talavera tiles.

Alluring: *añil* peeling off the courtyard
    terrace amid songbirds' warbles,

the chatter of parrots, the steely barks
    of hairless dogs, their skin slate-blue.

Always at dusk, Frida arrived home, beguiling,
    costumed in violet-blue.

The hall mirror reflected my longtime
    occupant, her indigo jewels, jangling,

her throaty laughter, euphoric, pouring
    out of windows into narrow streets

of Coyoacán, rushing into azure lakes,
    rivers, crossing borders—

a blue tapestry like a talisman falling from sky,
    even more seductive than before.

NEW POEMS

These Flecks of Color

"I know very well that not a single flower is drawn completely, that they are more dabs of colour, red, yellow, orange, green, blue, violet . . ."
                 Vincent van Gogh, Letter to Wilhelmina van Gogh,
                 31 July 1888

The fullness of sun permeates
         Silvery gray. The hue changes
the landscape where the painter stoops
         near a moss-colored field
to admire soil's sleek contours, slender rows
         of wild thyme – the pervading aroma
of red geraniums feverish in midday glare.
         in flickering shadows.
"I am hard to please," he whispers to himself.
         "I will paint nature's colors juxtaposed.
Rising, he embellishes sky with Veronese green
         I will hide clouds in a sweep of yellow.
so intense it floods a sunflower bed.
         It settles on leaf-wings of violets,
It flourishes beneath cypress trees.
         swaying in a distant breeze."
Never look at him with disdain for separating colors
         He places contrasting hues, side by side,
into flecks of ultramarine, orange, emerald.
         undulating near a square of bluebells.
When stipples encircle a trinity of flora,
         As sun falls under the stars' canopy,
when the dabs shimmer as a whole,
         the artist no longer longs for more.
he heads home wrapped in a pearl of light.

Painting in an Enclosed Field at Saint-Paul Hospital

After Vincent van Gogh's Landscape at Saint-Rémy (Enclosed Field with Peasant), 1889

"... *We, who live by bread, are we not ourselves very much like wheat ... to be reaped when we are ripe ....*"
          Vincent van Gogh, 1889

Like a peasant
        Devout,
I long to haul wheat
        we rise
in the fertile field, enclosed
        and billow
by the asylum's walls   I want
        in venerable breezes
to feel the gentle rocking of
        Roots
the gathered stalks
        unfurl, curl
A prism disperses ocher
        into pulsating soil
Lilac rays define
        Sinewy, we grow
olive trees, cypresses,
        like wild thyme, free
sheltered by the rugged Alpilles
        from the North's cold
In this enclosure I strive to recover
        We flower,
amid a wellspring of light
        the florets: aureate,
At the easel, I do for the wheat
        the stems: limber, sleek
what I have done for the reaper
        Sun-drenched, we spit seeds—

I breathe lissome air
        little eyes loosened —
and paint a peasant, hauling a bundle
        onto holy ground
Wary, my attendant follows me
        Our hearts bloom
wherever I go, earthy yellows,
        They ripen into braided gold
silvery grays, blues spattered
        Earth's tongue unfolds,
over my arms, outstretched
        lets go
like ripened grain
        its wind-borne song

Northern Lights

After Hans Grohs' Nordlicht, 1967

Do not fear the strange flicker
of indigo in polar skies

> *They call my brush strokes*
> *harsh as a Norse storm,*

or fiery slivers racing toward
earth in a glacial chill.

> *my demons darker*
> *than Edvard Munch's.*

Do not call us omens of war.
Fox fires. Bloody lichen on stone.

> *I fill canvasses with auroras:*
> *scrims of beryl blue.*

Honor our fluorescent curtains,
our arcs, and coronas of rays.

> *These mythic ribbons of color*
> *gleam with menace*

We will give you — come September —
a spirited dance. Praise us.

> *until I christen the rolling*
> *waters with dabs of gold,*

Come October, a rupture of mauve.
Come March, violet flung into the heavens.

> *cover night with translucence,*
> *and quell my trembling spirit.*

Come April, a verdant epiphany,
the slap of emerald flames,

> *I long for the islands of Lofoten,*
> *for the howling winds,*

a siren's call in night's icy glow.
With your mighty brush, give praise.

> *for the mystical borealis,*
> *its burnished song.*

Femme Fatale

After Georges de Feure's Window, ca. 1901–02

I wear silence to bait you,
        hands pillowed
beneath my chin,

a floral gown showy
        with a mermaid's
flounce and flare.

Like the moon, I wear
        seduction:
serpentine feathers

woven through a hat
        embellished
with a sparrow.

Its amorous song flits
        among orchids,
poppies, fleshy irises

that adorn my dress
        and climb the stone
wall I lean against.

Never turn your back
        on a lady
whose fragrance draws you

into smoky webs: umber,
        green, rose in the glint
and glare of glass.

In a garden of calla lilies
        opening, I beguile
you. With lead strips

I encircle your heart.
        Darkness soars
through an alluring sky.

Moonlight Marine

After Edward M. Bannister's Moonlight Marine, 1885

At dusk, mist lifts
      out of the ocean,
           surrounds clouds
      woven like a vow.

Tossed onto rocky
      shoals, waves
           unravel, undo
      all mockery of blue

as they glisten,
      then retreat
           toward a ship
      sailing to sea.

Ringed in gold, moon
      rises, discloses
           wanderings
      beyond the horizon:

whales trawling
      in speed-bursts
           with the freedom
      of wind, their roars

magnified as they tunnel
      the depths.
           I step into night,
      douse myself

in luminous froth
      until up I rise,
           spinning
      in a whirl of air.

Poplars on the Epte

After Claude Monet's *Poplars* Series

Lithe poplars tower into sky,
lure the floating boat like Lorelei.
Svelte, their wild berry reflections dye

the Epte turquoise, and at dusk: tiger's-eye
amber. The lunar hour settles, deifies
the trees, filigreed ribbons drawn on sky.

The artist sketches, his *modus operandi*
to remain afloat and apply
watery strokes until wavelets dry,

until leggy trees, mirrored, swing by
the boat predictably. Near fields of rye,
the poplars tower into a miniature sky,

lit by a brush full of ochre applied
so that elusive rays appear and dry
like stipples in glass, hand-blown by

artisans. Storms brew the hour the trees die,
chopped by a merchant from Limetz vying
for wood. The shorn limbs crash through lazuli
haze, hurling ripples into a shattered sky.

Seascapes

". . . in order to really paint the sea, you have to see it every day, at every hour and in the same place . . ."
  Claude Monet

I.   *Impression: Sunrise*

Imagine a fire's full brilliance
licking the sea: the morning's entrance,

imperial, and boaters in a trance
transfigured. Imagine the elegance

startling the couple, its wild radiance
caught off-center on the ripples' dance.

By chance, the painter comes upon this expanse,
the old harbor of Le Havre, France

giving gratitude for the hour, its resonance
stirring the lovers, the day's advance.

II.   *Rough Sea at Étretat*

Waves slap against cliffs:
gray caps angered as if

the artist painted them adrift,
unaware of their desire to be stylish, swift.

In its fury, the storm seems a gift
to render, but the rough swells stiffen

and confuse the painter: no sun lifts
overhead, something to learn about the drifting

waves, something sinister in the shifting
froth, scaling the cliffs.

III.   *The Beach at Sainte-Adresse*

Dozens of clouds, bedazzled, hang low
over a teal sea, drenched green in shadows.

Onlookers exchange *les bons mots*
while yachts, like distant strangers, go

eastward, unaffected by the day's slow
spirit. The beach, a makeshift studio,

pleases the artist painting *en plein air* as though
the boats, the fickle rays, a hidden rainbow

cast off doubts. For this favor, he owes
a debt to Sainte-Adresse and robes her aglow.

IV.   *Sunset at Étretat*

Wavelets of colored paint churn like butter
and carpet the billows, the cliff backlit, a blur

of blackened amethyst and beige. A barrister
sun pours orange onto rock and water,

holds court at dusk for the scavengers
of yellow speckling the distance: exotic liqueur.

On a whim, the artist hires
a boat to carry him over,

the waters clinging to day here
in Étretat, where his mind abolishes fear.

Claude Monet's Garden

The pink house dazzles.
    A green-shuttered window, closed
        like a bud, opens.

Irises en masse
    sing in a violet mist:
        nature's early Mass.

First water lily,
    a primitive Eve, pale white,
        turns to purest pink.

Melodious suite:
    Full sun on butterfly wings.
        Willful shadows stir.

Laden arches dare
    the horse chestnut trees to jump
        hurdles in the pond.

From a rose bouquet
    reds, lavenders loosen, fall
        as reflections, twirl.

Willows laugh and sway.
    Amused, they wave to their own
        light-hearted ripples.

The frail artist does
    not see, his eyes silenced by
        the sky's jeweled light.

O'Keeffe's Desert Terrain, Ghost Ranch

I.
Simplify the details, she reminds
      herself, the clay road undulating
            with heat, Chimney Rock

a stark cadence, a howl.
      Scanning the terrain, she watches
            the Pedernal unveil clouds.

The slanted cap rock reaches out,
      beckons the artist to sketch
            its frame as if it were a saint:

ancient, lordly, worthy of her ashes
      flung across its revered back.
            A ghostly sunset appears —

eternal fire she emulates.
      Flames soar behind cliffs,
            alter the throbbing design.

II.
Who cannot feel her presence woven
      into these wind-swept hills?
            Today she simplifies

a tree, its limbs petrified, curled
      like antlers on a ram's head,
            bleached bones

swallowed by a plush corridor
      of rays, by the steady sound
            of hawks swooping

down to observe the desolate
      landscape she draws: flat-topped
            mountain stripped bare

as if washed by rain, the desert
      disrobed — like a lover
            seen for the first time.

Evening Star

After Georgia O'Keeffe's Evening Star No. III, 1917

On a new moon night,
        she walks into darkness,
                calmed by beaming

teal streams. Circular rays
        lift her into space,
                vibrant as hills

rinsed in alpenglow.
        Crimson lakes soar
                around Evening Star:

A spirit god, the artist thinks,
        cup of Heaven flowing,
                taming a wild coyote's

howl so she can paint
        nature's inaudible
                chants caressing

a cottonwood's crown,
        the toothed limbs
                dispersing amber

over the artist's hands.
        Gathering a palmful
                of downy tuft,

she returns to the studio
        and captures
                the star's

euphoric flute-call
        drifting out of
                a halo of leaves.

Miracle Flower

After Georgia O'Keeffe's Jimson Weed, 1936

Jimson Weed, Devil's Snare,
        poisonous as lust,
release your beauty

into shadows, lure me
        under your spell.
Pricklyburr, Thorn Apple

odorous as oil, extend
        your green stems
and strong-scented leaves.

Unfurl your alabaster petals,
        restless as snow.
I don't need to taste

your venom — your small
        black seeds —
to walk among spirits

or commune with deities.
        Stunned, I watch
you wilt in the flare of day —

you, delirious for twilight,
        your night blooms,
a palace of desire.

With green and golden
        swirls, I stylize
your floral centers,

outline with nectar
        your angular lips
until translucent

with venerable heart,
        you fan out
rapturous in desert moon.

GEORGE WASHINGTON: MOUNT VERNON

I.   The Birth Night Ball

> *After Edward Percy Moran's painting,* George Washington Dancing the Minuet with Nellie Curtis in his Mt. Vernon Home, February 22, 1777

The general takes her hand and glides across the floor,
entranced by the minuet's light-hearted grace
while regal tones of violins and a cello soar.

The candles' flames adorn walls, sculpted doors.
They illuminate his partner's youthful face
as he lifts her hand and glides across the floor.

The lilt and sway of instruments call for
all to rise and dance — a hand's embrace,
each bow regal as the purest notes soar.

Tall, august, muscular as war,
the general commands the room, keeps pace
in *pas menus,* then glides across the floor.

Dispelling winter's scorn, he adores
these unpretentious, slender steps, a trace
of Bach, the lofty tones of violins as a cello soars.

His fair complexion, his blue-gray eyes score
admiration from ladies fanning their faces.
Enfolding his partner's hand, he glides across the floor.
The merry tones of violins and a cello soar.

II.   **A Midsummer Evening on the Piazza**

After Benjamin Henry Latrobe's painting, A View of Mount Vernon with the Washington Family, 1796

Shadows flit along the promontory
as two ships, ringed in setting sun,
sail by the mansion like a whisper.

The president retreats to the piazza,
to the comfort of bird calls
lifting out of manicured bushes.

Stately in a Windsor chair,
he relishes the mild breeze
sweeping through the columns,

this sheltered space: far from
the upheavals of a new nation.
Lady Washington and a child

look on as a playful spaniel
leaps in midair. A guest explores
the grounds through a spyglass

while Nelly, mesmerized
by a cardinal's slow trill,
leans against a wooden pillar,

the familiar notes of nature's
harpsichord ascending.
There are no imperfections

here as evening awakens,
the banquet: tea served
from a silver urn, no one

on this airy veranda missing
a thing, its solitude as quelling
as the Potomac's tidal flow.

III. **A Private Place**

> *Inspired by Washington's study and a portrait entitled,*
> Lawrence Washington, c. 1743

Every day, Washington awakes at sunrise,
retreats to the study, a sanctuary where
he composes letters, reads books. Astute, wise,

he seeks answers to crop rotation, ways to fertilize
farm fields, lessen reliance on tobacco, pair
wheat with corn. Each day he awakes at sunrise,

seeks solace in a room, where he analyzes
the nation's unrest, the effects of warfare.
He composes letters, reads books. Astute, wise,

he manages the estate, the outlying farms, advises
overseers, records expenses in a wooden chair.
Disciplined, he awakes at sunrise,

descends stairs to a haven, a place that belies
its strength: built-in bookcases, a desk where
he composes diary entries, letters. Astute, wise,

he finds solitude in a chamber hidden from skies,
in the portrait of Lawrence, lit-up like a prayer.
Every morning, Washington awakes at sunrise,
composes letters, reads books: astute, wise.

IV. The Final Battle, 1799

Inspired by Life of George Washington: The Christian, *lithograph by Claude Regnier, after Junius Brutus Stearns, 1953*

Astride his horse, he weathers snow,
hail, and rain, inspects his property

with a guardian's eye before returning
home, chilled and wet. He joins

guests for dinner, tells himself,
No need to change out of soaked attire,

having withstood far worse in war:
crossing the frozen Delaware,

enduring a harsh winter at Valley Forge.
His throat inflamed, he ventures forth

the next morning, marks trees to chop
down, later retreats to the study to read.

Hours pass. His condition worsens.
Neither bloodletting, nor a dosage

of vinegar, molasses, and butter reduces
the pain. Neither sage tea, nor additional

bleeding. Neither his wife's gentle touch,
nor the vigilance of doctors brings a cure.

I am not afraid to go, he says, candle flames
refulgent in darkness, the bedchamber

sanctified by portraits of granddaughters.
The next night at 10:20 p.m.

the president, an intrepid soldier,
takes his leave. Lady Washington

exits the room for the final time.
The door closes like a muffled sigh.

Dipping My Brush into Black

I see no victims, no rehab
centers for exploited youth.

I hear no children crying,
their love abused by strangers

in darkened rooms.
I stare long into white

until girls become clouds
racing out of troubled skies.

When I swirl my brush
through yellow, they

become incandescent sun.
There is no suffering

in the studio, no suffering
in a beryl-blue lake

where mistreated girls
swim again, seaweed

wrapping their limbs
in jeweled green.

In the studio, black
becomes onyx, sable,

a magnificent ebony horse.
I hoist a lavender flag

over the girls, the lake,
the stallion on the shore,

over all that blooms out of
the wilderness of myself.

Nine Lives

Like a cat, I've lived nine lives.
Nearly lost one to an infection,

another to a boozer.
Nothing but a ruse to be

fooled into dating a man
addicted to abusing.

Once I was saved by chance,
a late-night near-miss:

diesel truck barreling 80 mph
down a foggy country road.

In a Costa Rica cloud forest
I survived an earthquake.

Outran Hurricane Hazel
on the North Carolina coast.

Eluded a microburst, fierce
winds toppling ancient oaks.

Lost hearing in my ear
when a pilot downed the plane

unexpectedly in Santa Cruz.
On a godforsaken street

in Buenos Aires, I got held up
by robbers. Endured a 24-hour

drug-run flight from Lima to Caracas.
Call me unlucky, but call me shrewd.

I have more lives to live to outwit
fate at this cagey game.

Books

Whenever you puzzle over a book,
savor the soundboard of syllables

that croon like singers or trill like stars —
soggy peat of Ireland, *sacred assassin*:

a crow, *ruined trenches* of war,
soul sister blooming her way

into friendship. Savor translations,
lyrical, emblematic — *l'aire resplendent.*

Un viento estival. Let scholarly books
hammer insights about feminism

or pollution. To exorcize loneliness,
let poets soothe with lyrical lines.

Let mathematicians parade numbers
and equations until you master logic.

Let memoirists confess their secrets:
a blueprint of your own invisible scars.

Books are curious gods, thirsty
for the vastness of open plains.

Hold a bestseller up, admire its density,
its power to refuel with words layered

page on page like fine crystals,
humming the lessons of dawn.

Talisman for Discovery

"Solitude is the school of genius."
                                Edward Gibbon

With a hidden mirror held up to sun, solve
      a puzzle the universe whispers
            in a thousand tongues.

Flee to headwaters, a forested swamp, wild
      plum bursting into song. Unravel
            an intricate web. Catch intrigue

by kayaking, the tap-tap of your paddle,
      a prod beyond the da Vincis,
            Einsteins, van Goghs, Bachs.

Paddle until inner voices rise like chants,
      wavering on the surface. Paddle long
            and linger until shadows pour

from mouths of egrets hidden in thickets
      of dusk. Let darkness soar
            until the mire's soil serenades

you, lost in abandon among royal ferns
      and wondering why it took so long
            to let the mind go,

to let it spin at will, vibrating
      in midair — an echo in the ease
            of a solitary swamp.

Tinnitus

The ringing like a claw starts,
        a sequestered racket
                that hisses in sleep

and hums in a spring-fed swamp,
        spatterdock's *clair de lune* hearts
                bobbing like vessels.

Easing my kayak beyond the stream's
        fringe, I paddle through
                the after-hush of dusk.

Feverish, the stars. The moon coy
        above a quilt of clouds,
                the wetlands in an uproar—

owls, raccoons, minks sounding
        an alarm as jarring as a howl
                in the hoarse throat

of night. The feathery dark swells
        to a crescendo, a choir
                of spring peepers

in search of mates. Lowering
        my head, I count the times
                their vocal sacs fill

and empty, these cross-bearers
        olive-green, tan and gray,
                colors I see every time

my ear whistles. The din—
        the maddening noise—calms
                among the scent

of half-opened cow lilies,
        seductive in these elusive
                headwaters.

O canopy of bald cypress,
      sycamore, sweetgum,
            dance for me

until my hearing heals
      in the defining hour,
           windless, serene.

Fireflies

In the 1950s the signature flashes
lured us outdoors to bottle a multitude

of tiny constellations. Flickering
beneath the Northern Cross, they

courted mates, swarmed, shot by us
like fire bolts, their lit bellies flaring.

Circling trees, they flew out
of our grasp. Chasing the beams,

we raced, woozy, through the yard,
caught a jarful, studied the rapid

code-like blinks. Mesmerized, we
unscrewed the lids, set the sky aflame.

*

Where is the on-off shimmer
that once enthralled us? A firefly

flits through blistering air, its glow
signaling a Morse code. Landing

on my fingertips, its beacon comes
alive in the mind of a young girl

twisting open a Mason jar to free
the insect's yellow-green sheen.

What has gotten into us?
Everywhere lanterns and porch

globes drown the mating call,
marsh grasses sprayed, fields

sheared, habitats gone. Standing
by the cove's edge, I recall a place

where hundreds once flooded the banks.
Someone shake us before it's too late.

In Polar Waters

At daybreak, whales hoist
        their smooth,
               tapered
        bodies into air, emit

deafening groans as ships
        swirl in for the kill,
               harpoon
        cannons exploding.

Marbled like florescent
        opals, krill graze
               the surface
        as the colossal

mammals circle in pairs,
        toss spume
               onto shoals,
        drench glacial shores

with tunneling roars.
        Supple swimmers,
               they trawl
        currents, escape

an avalanche of grenades,
        outwit fishermen
               in a wave-dance.
        While the world far away

sleeps, they wail, their songs
        plaintive like futile
               prayers echoing
        deep in the ocean's throat.

Have Mercy

on us for spraying the kitchen
counters and floors with toxins.

Have mercy on our children,
who romp through polluted streams.

Show mercy to silkworms
annihilated from cornfields.

To homes lit by wildfires,
fueled by Santa Ana winds.

Be merciful to coastlands torn
asunder by the likes of Rita, Ike.

To dead zones: shrouded graves
of oysters, crabs, and shad.

Be merciful to glaciers, to polar
bears clinging to chunks of ice.

To us for smothering
our bodies with poisonous

creams and lotions, for lathering
our lips with petroleum.

Have mercy on our kidneys
and livers, scarred by boozing.

On pain pills that wound us.
On tap water that sickens us.

On our choice to go on living
like this: Have mercy.

Peace Offering

The citizens must have been sleeping
when bombs rained on Rouen, the Law Courts'

flamboyant façade impervious to its riddled past.
I reflect back to the late 40s. A child then,

I loved roses, red-flamed like holly berries.
I came to France this week to escape the reminder

of America's plane-bombings, to find peace
among half-timbered houses and stone cathedrals.

It's hard to pull away from this square, my mind
slow to digest horror on a scale this grand.

I had not been born when shrapnel scarred
this building, gouging giant holes, some large enough

to protect birds. The Courts with their pinnacles
and flying buttresses transform into angry flames

across the ocean, the afterglow of steel veiled
in smoke like blackened stars. War is like this:

*Earth suspended. A scented rose dangling
in abeyance. Why not otherwise? Earth*

in abeyance. A rose releasing its fragrant cure.
I pull back from wintry weather shrouding my thoughts.

Starting over, I enter a constellated Rouen,
holiday lights arched over streets, the Courts a prelude

to ornate churches, every window candled,
my spirit uplifted to a place where I gather

childhood roses, and hold one upright, emblazoned,
as I look back on my perfect world.

NOTES & GLOSSARY

CONTRARY VISIONS

"Contrary Visions in the Gallery, *White on White*"
The epigraph, which expresses Italian painter Piero Manzoni's intention to rid his canvases of all symbolism and connotation, is printed here in its entirety – "a white that is not a polar landscape, not a material in evolution or a beautiful material, not a sensation or a symbol or anything else: just a white surface that is simply a white surface and nothing else." [From Herbert Read, *A Concise History of Modern Painting,* Oxford University Press, 1974, p. 308].

"From the Cloister, Saint-Rémy"
Vincent van Gogh was confined for extreme depression during the last year of his life (1889 –1890) to Saint-Paul Asylum in Saint-Rémy-de-Provence. At this time he disagreed vehemently with painters Paul Gauguin and Emile Bernard about the aims of art. From *The Letters of Vincent van Gogh,* edited by Mark Roskill (New York: Atheneum, 1970, p. 328): " . . . The thing is that I have worked this month in the olive groves, because they [Bernard and Gauguin, who had sent records of their recent work] have maddened me with their Christs in the Garden, with nothing really observed."

Van Gogh and his beloved brother Theo corresponded on a weekly basis for nearly ten years (1880 – 1890). Their correspondence is preserved in *The Letters of Vincent van Gogh.*

"Crows over the Fields of Auvers"
Vincent van Gogh's painting, *Wheat Field with Crows,* completed shortly before the artist committed suicide in 1890, is the basis for this poem. Meyer Schapiro in *Vincent van Gogh* (Doubleday & Company, Inc., 1980, p. 130) presents this description of the painting: "The singular format of the canvas is matched by the vista itself, a field opening out from the foreground by way of three diverging paths . . . these end blindly in the field or run out of the picture . . . . The blue sky and the yellow fields pull away from each other with

disturbing violence; across their boundary, a flock of black crows advances toward the unsteady foreground."

"Nude Descending in All Directions"
This poem emerged after viewing Marcel Duchamp's painting, *Nude Descending the Stairs.* Duchamp said about his painting: "It is an organization of kinetic elements, an expression of time and space through the abstract presentation of motion . . . ." (Herbert Read, *A Concise History of Modern Painting,* p. 113).

The aim of the Dada art movement was to shock the bourgeoisie – whom the Dadaists blamed for World War I – by breaking up conventional notions of art as Duchamp did in his reproduction of Mona Lisa with a moustache.

"The Mathematical Bridge, Cambridge"
The Mathematical Bridge, located at Cambridge University in England, was designed by Sir Isaac Newton and built in 1749 – 1750. Held together by calculated strains, with no nails or bolts to mar the russet-colored beams, the fabled bridge arcs across the River Cam linking the medieval brick buildings of Queens' College to the Back Greens.

"I Don't Know Why I Wake Up Angry"
St. Elizabeths Hospital is a psychiatric hospital, located in southeast Washington, D.C.

GATHERING LIGHT

"As a Teacher I'm Inclined to Ignore the Critics"
In her article, "Cather and O'Keeffe: Spirits of the Southwest," Polly Duryea tells us that O'Keeffe painted *The Lawrence Tree* after a visit to Lady Dorothy Brett at D.H. Lawrence's ranch in New Mexico. [From: *Kansas Quarterly.* Vol. 19. No. 4. 1987, p. 33.] O'Keeffe's rendition of the skeletal tree resembles a cross in that the top branches part, resting horizontally against a blue sky studded with stars. The tree is emphasized through perspective: the viewer stands at the tree's base and looks skyward through its branches.

O'Keeffe frequently painted the Pedernal, a mountain near the *Rancho de los Burros* close to the Ghost Ranch complex in New Mexico. About this flat-topped mountain, she said: "It's my private mountain. It belongs to me. God told me if I painted it enough, I could have it." [From: Lisle, Laurie. *Portrait of an Artist: A Biography of Georgia O'Keeffe.* New York: Washington Square Press. 1980, p. 299.]

Horse's Skull with White Rose, oil on canvas, painted in 1931

"Above Clouds"

In line 2, "a Z waving its curvaceous tail" refers to O'Keeffe's painting, *Winter Road I,* 1963.

In lines 2-3, "an *altiplano* of clouds" refers to the series, *Sky Above Clouds,* 1963.

Abiquiu, New Mexico: the site of O'Keeffe's Ghost Ranch where she spent most of her summers after 1934

chimaja: a sweet-smelling herb

In line 15, "the moon sanctified a cache of white bones" refers to *Pelvis with Shadows and the Moon,* 1943.

In line 17, "shells and skulls" refers to *White Shell with Red,* 1938; *Red Hill and White Shell,* 1938; *From the Faraway Nearby,* 1937.

In line 18, "a single poppy, a calla lily, her ranch door" refers to *Red Poppy,* 1927; *Lily – White with Black,* 1927; *My Last Door,* 1934; *White Patio with Red Door,* 1960.

In line 23, "a jack-in-the-pulpit" refers to *Jack-in-the-Pulpit, No. III,* 1930.

"Balloon Safari over Masai Mara"
Masai Mara (also Maasai Mara) is a wildlife reserve, located in southwest Kenya.

"Among the Ruins of Puca Pucara, Perú"
Puca Pucara: The Red Fortress, used in Inca times to protect the surrounding temples and water reserves. Today Indian children wander the ruins in search of money or "gifts" from tourists.

ichu: a grass of the upper Andes used for forage or thatching

"Machu Picchu"
Machu Picchu (also spelled Macchu Picchu, Spanish; and Macchupicchu, Quechua)

olluco (also *ullucu*, the Quechua spelling) is a root crop grown high in the Andes.

quínua (also *quínoa*, Spanish and Quechua spelling) is a grain crop of the Andean highlands rich in protein.

Puente Ruinas literally means "the point of the ruins." The train carrying passengers to the fabled ruins stops in Puente Ruinas at the foot of the peak where Machu Picchu is located.

Intihuatana: sundial

"Christmas in Bolivia"
Inti: the sun god of the Andean Indians
Catorce de Septiembre: the central plaza of Cochabamba, Bolivia
boliviano: Bolivian currency
quena: Indian flute

"Mariano Quispe"
The impetus for this poem was an article about Mariano Quispe, a *quipu camayoc* from the Andean hamlet Micaypata. According to author Loren McIntyre, Quispe uses the *quipu*, "a series of knotted strings," to account for the "crop and livestock production for each man in his hamlet." McIntyre continues: "More elaborate *quipus* served the Incas, whose culture lacked written numerals as well as the written word. With a decimal system, royal statisticians kept track of such vital data as births, deaths, weapons, and food. Colors of yarn, knots and the turns within a knot all related various information . . . . Each *quipu-keeper* might have hundreds of *quipus* coiled and stored in jars. But only professionally trained *quipu* 'rememberers' could interpret the knots. Today, no one can tell what the silent strings recorded." [From: McIntyre, Loren. *The Incredible Incas and their Timeless Land*. Washington, D.C.: The National Geographic Society. 1975, p. 30.]

chicha: a fermented corn liquor drink made by the Andean Indians

DEATH COMES RIDING

"Mother"
Sagrada Família: the celebrated church of noted architect, Antoni Gaudí. Located in Barcelona, Spain, the building, still unfinished, is the city's greatest Modernista accomplishment. At night, illuminated, the church assumes an ethereal appearance.

"Ice Maiden"
In the spring of 1996, the mummy, called Juanita, was on display for a month in the National Geographic Society's Explorers Hall, where I viewed the exhibit and attended a lecture by Dr. Reinhard, who discussed the circumstances of his rare discovery.

"Elena Mesa"
Elena's doctor, Count Karl von Cosel, lived with her remains for seven years. After his secret was discovered, Elena was buried in an undisclosed area in the island's cemetery [Rod Bethel. *A Halloween Love Story*].

"The Quechuan Boy of Cuzco"
anticuchos: shish kebabs generally made of pork hearts
toyo: a folkloric wind instrument

"Azucena's Arpillera"
arpillera: a folkloric wall hanging, handmade by Andean Indians to recount their histories

chicharrón: crackling of pork

chicha: a fermented corn liquor drink

quena, zampoña: wind instruments of the Andean highlands

maíz: corn

pututu: a conch shell which sounds like a haunting horn

ichu: a grass of the upper Andes used for forage or thatching

"A Basket of Potatoes"
chuño: freeze-dried potatoes

"Song to the Sun God, Inti"
espiritú del Lago Titicaca, regalo de la Isla del Sol: spirit of Lake Titicaca, gift of the Island of the Sun

Yungus: located less than 60 miles from La Paz, a sub-tropical region in Bolivia characterized by its lush fields and valleys

borsalinos: a type of hat worn by Indian women

maíz y las papas: corn and potatoes

Río Urubamba: located in Peru, the highest tropical river in the world

mariposas: butterflies

llamas, vicuñas, guanacos: Andean animals of the camel family

quenas, zampoñas: wind instruments of the Andean highlands

Huascar: a ruler of the Incan Empire

Regalo amarillo. Espiritú de todas: Yellow gift. Spirit of us all.

GREATEST HITS 1981 –2000

"Donna Bruna"
donna bruna: dark lady

femina scura: obscure woman

"The Replica"
The replica referred to in this poem is Queen Mary's Dolls' House presented to Queen Mary as a token of national goodwill. The Dolls' House is currently on display at Windsor Castle in England.

"Do You Know about the Rain Tree?"
The impetus for this poem came from reading two articles by *The Washington Post* reporter, Eugene Robinson, who cites the following myth of the Yanomami Indians as told to him by Rev. Carlo Zacquini: "Do you know about the raintree? They say that there is an invisible tree with a very broad canopy in the sky, and that when its flowers mature, they fall to earth, as raindrops." [Robinson, Eugene. "Stone Age Crumbling." *The Washington Post.* June 24, 1991, p. A16.]

Beehive tombs: Located near Mycenae in Greece, these astounding tombs lay concealed for years, thought instead to be grassy hills. The vaulted, circular chambers open onto smaller burial chambers.

RIVER COUNTRY

"Dragon Run"
The Dragon Run, a 1-million-year-old bald cypress swamp, is an endangered ecological gem, located in Virginia's Middle Peninsula.

"The Jenny Dawn"
Tangier Island: a Chesapeake Bay island, considered the most remote spot in Virginia. Residents still rely on nearby oyster and crab grounds for their livelihood.

watermen: a term that refers to the men and woman who make their living by fishing, crabbing, and oystering on the Chesapeake Bay.

peeler: a crab nearly ready to shed its shell.

buster: a crab that has begun to shed its shell.

soft-shell: a crab that has shed its old shell, but hasn't yet formed a new shell.

deadrise: a cross-planked, wooden workboat built with a V-shaped bottom at the bow. Because of its unique design, the deadrise, developed around the 1880s, is suited to the shallows of the Chesapeake Bay. More recently, the boat has also been used to transport pleasure seekers on fishing trips. The deadrise is the official state boat of Virginia.

Hazel: a hurricane which struck the Atlantic coast of North America in 1954. According to Larry Chowning, author of several books on Chesapeake Bay life and lore, "Hazel was unique in that it literally sucked water out of the rivers, creeks, coves and guts of the Chesapeake Bay region," resulting "in three years of historical high catches on the Rappahannock River." [From: Chowning, Larry. "Plenty of Local Oysters for this Year's Festival." *Southside Sentinel.* November 2, 2006, C13, C15.]

"Hurricane"
consagrada a Dios: consecrated to God—the literal meaning of the name Isabel.   In 2003 Hurricane Isabel decimated the river country region of Virginia with a series of microbursts that uprooted trees and inundated homes in flood plains.

THE EMBRACE: DIEGO RIVERA AND FRIDA KAHLO

DIEGO RIVERA—1886-1957

[1]The epigraph that introduces the first section of the book is from Diego Rivera's *My Art, My Life: An Autobiography* (with Gladys March). New York: Dover Publications, Inc., 1991, p. 41. (ISBN: 0-486-26938-8)

"Diego and Calla Lilies": after *Calla Lily Vendor (Vendedora de alcatraces),* 1943 and *Nude with Calla Lilies (Desnudo con alcatraces), 1944.* Rivera painted the calla lily so often in connection with women that the flower became an erotic or sensual symbol in his art.

peso: unit of currency

petate: reed

"Halley's Comet":

Porfirio Díaz: dictator of Mexico (1877-1880 and 1884-1911)

Carmen Romero Rubio de Díaz: wife of Porfirio Díaz

muy importante: very important

la crema de la sociedad: the cream of the society

Angelina Beloff: Rivera's common-law wife with whom he lived in Europe from 1911-1921. Beloff gave birth to a son, Diego in 1916. Two years later the son died.

Marevna Vorobiev-Stebelska: Rivero left Beloff for six months in 1917 to live with Marevna, who gave birth to his daughter, Marika, in 1919.

campesinos: peasants; countrymen; farmers; Indians

MURALS
(Location: Secretaría de Educación Pública in Mexico City, Mexico)

"Entering the Mine": after *Entering the Mine (Entrada a la mina)*, Court of Labor, 1923

mi padre: my father

"Leaving the Mine": after *Leaving the Mine (Salida de la mina)*, Court of Labor, 1923

"Hymn: The Embrace": after *The Embrace (El abrazo)*, Court of Labor, 1923

mis hermanos: my brothers

"Offerings, Day of the Dead": after *The Sacrificial Offering, Day of the Dead (La ofrenda, Día de muertos)*, Court of the Fiestas, 1923-24

Posada: José Guadalupe Posada was an influential Mexican artist known for his *calaveras,* or sugar skulls, associated with the festival, Day of the Dead. His most famous creation is Calavera Catrina.

pescado y pollo picante: fish and spicy chicken

danza de la muerte: dance of death

"Bread": after *Our Bread (El pan nuestro)*, Court of the Fiestas, 1928

[2]The epigraph is from *Guia de los Murales de Diego Rivera en la Secretaría de Educación Pública.* Text by Antonio Rodriguez. 1986, p. 95.

pan rustico: rustic-style Spanish bread

WIVES

[3]The epigraph that introduces "Wives" is from Diego Rivera's *My Art, My Life: An Autobiography* (with Gladys March). New York: Dover Publications, Inc., 1991, p. 83. (ISBN: 0-486-26938-8)

"Angelina Beloff" and **"Lupe Marín"**: Both poems are monologues loosely inspired by comments attributed to Rivera's common-law wife and his second wife. [From: Rivera, Diego. *My Art, My Life: An Autobiography* (with Gladys March), Appendix, pp. 183-186.]

Lupe Marín: also known as Guadalupe Marín

"Frida Kahlo":
sapo-rana: toad-frog, one of Kahlo's affectionate nicknames for Rivera

"Emma Hurtado":
El Popo: the abbreviated form of *Popocatépetl*, an active volcano, southeast of Mexico City.
Guanajuato: the town of Diego's birth, known for its silver mines.

FRIDA KAHLO: 1907-1954

[4]The epigraph for the second section of the book is from a statement Frida Kahlo made to reporters of *Time* magazine on the occasion of her first solo exhibition in Mexico in 1953 (*Galería de Arte Contemporáneo*). [From: Zamora, Martha. *Frida Kahlo: The Brush of Anguish*. Trans. Marilyn Sode. San Francisco: Chronicle Books LLC, ©1990, p. 126. Used with permission of Marquand Books, Inc., Seattle, WA]

"Frida and Wet Nurse": after *My Nurse and I (Mi nana y yo)*, 1937

"The Wedding Fiesta": Kahlo and Rivera married on August 21, 1929.

Pieter Brueghel (also Bruegel): a 16th century Flemish painter
rebozo: wrap; shawl
mole: black chili sauce
las dos Fridas: the two Fridas

"The Two Fridas (I): On the Border Line between Mexico and the United States": after *Self-Portrait on the Border Line between Mexico and the United States (Autorretrato en la frontera entre México y Estados Unidos)*, 1932

gringolandia: the United States

"The Two Fridas (II): Collage, Manhattan": after *My Dress Hangs There (Mi vestido cuelga ahí)*, 1933

"The Two Fridas (III): Sitting on Wicker Bed with Ceramic Doll": after *Self-Portrait on the Bed* or *Me and My Doll (Yo y mi muñeca)*, 1937

"Frida Dialogues with Her Heart": after *Memory, or the Heart (Recuerdo)*, 1937

"The Two Fridas (IV)": after *The Two Fridas (Las dos Fridas)*, 1939

"The Two Fridas (V): The Wounded Table": after *The Wounded Table (La mesa herida)*, 1940

"The Two Fridas (VI): Broken Column and Plaster Cast": after *Broken Column (La columna rota)*, 1944 and *Plaster Cast with Hammer and Sickle (La escayola con la hoz y el martillo)*, 1950

fragmentos: fragments

"The Two Fridas (VII): Paint Me Flying": after *Feet What Do I Need Them for if I Have Wings to Fly (Pies, para qué los quiero si tengo alas pa' volar)*, 1953, an illustration in Kahlo's diary. [Note: Only one leg was amputated below the knee.]

[5]The epigraph comes from *THE DIARY OF FRIDA KAHLO*. English translation copyright ©2005. New York: Harry N. Abrams, Inc., p. 277. Used by permission of Harry N. Abrams, Inc., New York. All rights reserved.

mandrake root: considered a cure for infertility

Píntame volando: Paint me flying

"Letter to Diego": This poem was inspired by Kahlo's *Accident (Accidente)*, 1926; *Self-Portrait with Her Hair Cut Off (Autorretrato de pelona)*, 1940; *Self-Portrait with Plait (Autorretrato con trenza)*, 1941; and by Rivera's *Epic of the Mexican People (Epopeya del pueblo mexicano)* in the fresco cycle, 1929-35.

Tehuana dress: Kahlo wore the native garb of the Isthmus of Tehuantepec to please Diego, who valued her indigenous heritage. The ruffled skirt hid her leg shriveled by polio. The embroidered blouse completed the elegant costume.

Nahui Olín: one of Diego's models

"The Crematorium at the Panteón Civil de Dolores":
huipiles: embroidered blouses

"La Casa Azul":
añil: indigo

retablos: altarpieces

Coyoacán: a suburb of Mexico City, where Kahlo lived for most of her life in the Blue House, or *La Casa Azul*

NEW POEMS

"Seascapes": Claude Monet's four paintings that inspired the sections of "Seascapes" are *Impression: Sunrise; Rough Sea at Étretat; The Beach at Sainte-Adresse;* and *Sunset at Étretat.*

"Talisman for Discovery" was presented at the 2008 Phi Beta Kappa Induction Ceremony at the University of Mary Washington.

Made in the USA
Middletown, DE
10 January 2019